The TOWN GARDEN

First published in Great Britain in 1989 by
Exley Publications Ltd
16 Chalk Hill, Watford, Herts WD1 4BN, United Kingdom.
First published in Belgium by H. Dessain, Liege, Belgium
Copyright © 1987. All rights reserved.

Translation copyright © Exley Publications Ltd, 1989
Cover illustration copyright © Atelier Perspective, 1987

British Library Cataloguing in Publication Data
Vielle, Eliane.
    The town garden.
    1.   Town gardens. Planning – Amateurs' manuals.
    I.   Title.
    II.   Mon jardin de ville. *English*
    712'.6

ISBN 1-85015-208-X

Translation: Ros Schwartz Translations.
Editorial: Helen Exley and Margaret Montgomery.
Design: Agence FORUM, Brussels.
Typeset by Brush Off Studios, St Albans, Herts AL3 4PH.
Printed and bound in Hungary.

The TOWN GARDEN

Getting to know it
improving it
and enjoying it

Eliane Vielle

illustrations by Anne Lernout

CONTENTS

CONTENTS

Introduction

With the threat to the environment now one of the major problems facing us all, this book by Eliane Vielle is very timely. For eight years she has worked to make a desolate, bleak piece of city land into a green oasis visited by a host of different birds and butterflies. She believes, passionately, that our towns and cities can provide breathing space for embattled species, and that no plot of land, no window box, no wall or terrace garden is too small to ignore.

The good news is that her book demonstrates that a _balance_ of nature not only supports wildlife – it also creates the prettiest and most varied gardens.

Gathering about her experts on architecture, natural habitats, pond life and other specialities, she sets before us a feast of ideas for the greening of our own personal plots of earth, showing how to use shade, ground cover, indigenous plants, scented plants, each in their place in the scheme of things.

Then, with diagrams and tables, she shows even the most lazy gardener how to do it all – how to select the right plants for the right spot of the garden, how to choose the natural survivors, how to work with Nature instead of against her.

It's a beautiful book, with a wealth of ideas. We hope you enjoy it!

HIDDEN TREASURES.

I live in the middle of a large city in an old house with a small hundred-year-old garden.

Since I have lived here I have discovered many of its natural charms. In many ways I have found that I discovered more of nature's secrets here than I did during the times I have spent in the country.

Against the garden wall a few steps from the entrance to my garden stands a very old pear tree. It must once have been an espalier, but years of neglect have transformed it into a tall tree. Its bare branches bow over both sides of the wall. When I first saw it, a pale winter sun lightened the dark cracks in the bark and shone on a short brown coat of a little bat numb with cold.

His unexpected presence captivated and charmed me, and so I bought the house. I have never seen the little bat there again, although at nightfall, after the birds have stopped singing, I've seen him flying swiftly and gracefully through the air.

Friendly jays.

But every season the garden brings new joys. As I warm myself in front of the fire, I can look through to my garden on a snowy winter's morning, and I notice that

a couple of jays are suddenly getting friendly. It's all because I have hung a bag of peanuts on the lilac tree for the blue tits. They take it in turns to hook their beaks in and pull. Startled by the loud rattle of the window catch, they fly away. Blue tits, who were frightened away by the rude intrusion of the jays, return following one another performing endless somersaults.

Return of the drone and the solitary bee.

At the sight of the first crocuses, the bees make their return, inspecting each new messenger of spring: daffodil, narcissus, hyacinth.

Sometimes a little robin makes a rare appearance. A wise bird, he quietly shelters in the bushes catching insects and then, all of a sudden disappears.

On very cold days local blackbirds make themselves at home on the compost heap, rummaging for food to make up for their loss of body weight. Sometimes they are joined by the odd starling in speckled, winter feathers which can lead to short-lived noisy squabbles.

The ladybird ball.

After the frosts have disappeared, armies of red and yellow ladybirds with black spots reappear on the early buds and the first clumps of green. Each day at dawn, they begin their activity anew, feeding on microscopic organisms.

The silver birch is soon covered in small shoots and is visited by tired blue tits and a few sparrows which have returned.

Bright spring blossom.

When the trees are still only pale green, the peach tree suddenly bursts into blossom with a profusion of pretty pink flowers. The cherry tree and pear tree soon follow suit. This symphony of pink and white marks the beginning of spring. Bees, their legs full of pollen, are spoilt for choice. And there is a whole range of mottled, striped and furry insects.

The song of the nightingale.

What a strange coincidence! At daybreak on March 21 this year, the first day of spring, just on the terrace near the half-open French windows, where my terracotta pots are already sprouting shoots, the first song of the nightingale came to me. The song is still quiet and timid and it will soon be the turn of the blackbirds.

The terrace is bathed in early morning sun. What is this twittering bird who keeps rummaging in the flower pots leaving traces of spattered earth on the wall? There is just time to glimpse him before he darts into the bushes.

A bird which I am unable to identify has made its nest at the

top of the nearby hawthorn. And what about the bird in the bird box in the corner of the garden? In a few days she will be hidden amid a profusion of pink flowers.

The blackbird has started hunting for earthworms. He is unaware of the cat's presence and with his beak tears his prey into little pieces and eats it morsel-by-morsel before flying away.

The return of the swallows.

Two passing turtle doves meet in the heart of a large cherry tree. When they are not cooing they eat numerous little green cherries.

Swallows fly high above the rooftops uttering faint cries. They will soon find a place to nest.

Among alpine clematis, a bird box is providing shelter this year for a family of great tits.

Different shades of green.

There is every shade of green and each day there is a subtle change as spring advances. The first primroses open just as the last tulips shed their petals. Sweet cicely unfurls its white petals. Then it's the turn of the iris to flower. The spiraea produces a creamy cascade of flowers. Branches of the fruit trees bend over slightly under the weight of the blossom.

Chervil adds the taste of summer to our soup. We use a few dandelion and burnet leaves in our salad and in the evening we make a delicious fresh mint tea.

Birdsong.

Every day the birds sing non-stop. How lovely it is to be woken up by the dawn chorus!

Five o'clock in the afternoon is the time for another choral song. Blackbirds sing their couplets perched on the roof tops before flying off into the thicket. They flit from tree-to-tree under the watchful eye of the tomcat who stops for a moment before continuing his solitary prowl.

Everything becomes silent. All you can hear is the mewing of the cats chasing each other in the copse. From time to time you can hear the cry of a barn owl from an abandoned attic.

OUR GARDENS ARE OUR OWN NATURE RESERVES.

In the streets and avenues of every city there are little square islands of green surrounded by buildings. Behind these buildings are old, private gardens. Their age usually depends on how close they are to the middle of town. Divided by walls or hedges, they form a green oasis where natural life can bring us some peace and counter some of the effects of pollution and the excesses of town development.

Those who haven't a clue.

Many city dwellers have no idea

of the natural beauty they could enjoy. Some house fronts have been painted and to make their garden look tidy (and to keep up with the Jones's garden next door) people take down those "messy" climbing plants. The walls have been tiled with garish patterns or painted a pretty shade of orange – guaranteed indelible and washable! Everywhere patches of cement are covering the green.

Other people adore flowers, but are only coaxed into action with the arrival of spring. The rest of the year the garden goes unnoticed, except for the dog who makes puddles on the last living plants. In the summer, it's overgrown and in the winter it's trampled down, muddy and miserable.

Spring is the time when enthusiasm for gardening seems to be at its peak. Some people

become so enthusiastic that they chop down the remaining trees to make way for their vegetables. But the vegetables will be scraggy because the tree in the next garden is out of reach and will cast its shadow over them. That's a sore point – and now the birds have disappeared, too.

Here there was a tiny green garden with a good southerly aspect. On the wall you could see the foliage of an enormous lime tree.

Opposite, the high wall of a building was covered in ivy, but in this little garden the newcomer tore out the green, cleaned the walls and painted them a brilliant white. The ground is now covered in crazy paving that he'd wanted to soften with pot plants. But he didn't have time for those, so now little wisps of green grass are poking up through the paving and the small patio is rather sad and dirty.

Those who are neglectful.

The walls of the nearby garden are

crumbling after a wet winter. They have fallen on a thuja bush which was used to cover up the wall. It's sad about the bush; but there were too many thujas against that wall anyway. The new occupant is rather lazy and has not tended his little garden. It is becoming increasingly overgrown and is starting to resemble a small jungle.

Tired of trying to solve the problem of his wall falling down, he has put up a fence made of old assorted boards and behind this

he dumps all his rubbish from the cellar.

One lady has a small garden facing north-west. She believed that the old cherry tree at the end of the garden was depriving her of sunlight. In late spring she battled to saw off the top of the tree apart from two branches she could not reach and which are still sticking out stupidly. In fact the garden is just as gloomy; the cherry tree acted as a charming filter for the evening sun!

The end of a paradise.

The largest and most beautiful garden in the area was the work of a flower seller and his wife in the nineteenth century. It had many different species of plants with contrasting foliage intermingled with fruit trees, such as a huge apple tree which blossomed beautifully in the spring.

The garden gradually became overgrown from years of neglect,

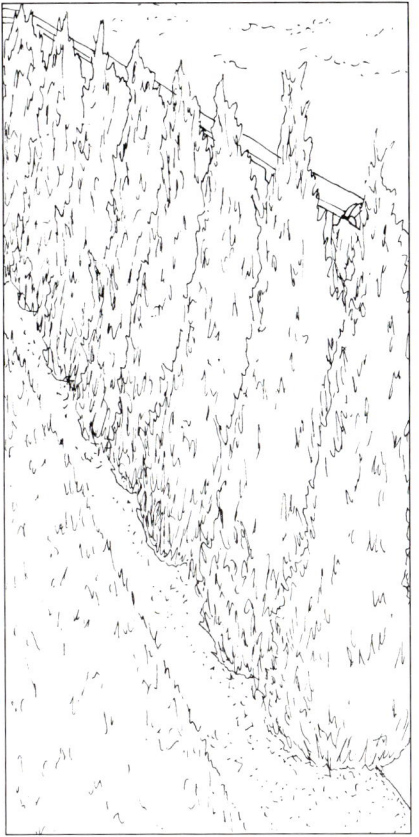

for on her daily walks the old woman only just about managed to pull out tree seedlings which had started to grow here and there. The old woman died and the house was bought by a fashionable couple who wanted to build a swimming pool in the garden.

They first set to work by tackling the old apple tree which lost its crown of spring blossom, while in the rest of the garden the ornamental trees were becoming increasingly overgrown.

In late spring, when all the flowers were in full blossom and the birds, enjoying the unusually dense foliage had built their nests among the plants and bushes, these new owners decided to "clean up" and cleared that part of the garden nearest the house.

They pulled down most of the bushes and built a bonfire. This space was probably going to be used as a dance floor for a birthday party or some such occasion. But the couple moved to a better house before that happened.

There's still a sad empty area in the middle of the garden. Birds, driven away by this merciless destruction, leave to find other bushes in the "neglected" area of the garden where some trees are still growing.

What will become of our little nature reserves?

How many species of birds will disappear?

How will we all live in a few years time if this destruction continues?

WHAT ARE WE TO DO?

To help us in this long task of re-introducing nature into our town gardens, I went to see the work of scientists who have started to plant a quantity of forgotten or rare species. They started in a patch of earth that had nothing – just like a small patch of town garden. What they have achieved is really inspiring.

A nursery with a difference.

We went to a remote area of the countryside near to closed-down collieries where very little grows. We drove along a road between cultivated fields – all the same with no trees or hedgerows. In the middle of this monotonous landscape a couple of acres were being used to develop a quite different kind of nursery. The oldest trees were only seven years old. As we entered our eyes were met by a curtain of wisteria in pale yellow, pink, violet and mauve. Attracted by these flowers, bees and insects abounded. Opposite, a paulownia tree opened its violet petals in the form of perfumed trumpets. The tree hung over a pond surrounded by a fence held in position by huge boulders. Yellow irises also hung over the water

covered in aquatic plants and teeming with life inside.

A great variety of bushes and hedges with delicate foliage lined either side of the pathway. We walked along all the paths looking at all the different flower-beds. The air was thick with the sound of birds and insects. It was truly beautiful.

Further along we could see beds of seedlings appearing among the shadows cast by the trees. Year-old currant bushes were covered in green leaves. Only a few clusters of currants remained.

"The bush has been attacked by caterpillars which have eaten nearly all the berries in just a few hours," we were told by the architect of this garden. "It's not a problem though, the bushes still need to be cut back.

"Pests are not as bad as they are made out to be. They are not really very damaging in an area where there are so many different species because pests cancel each other out."

I asked him what the birds thought of all these delicious-looking insects.

"The birds seem to come to my vegetable garden in increasing numbers. I keep noticing different species. In the morning it's a delight to hear the dawn chorus. The pond also seems to attract certain birds. Even migratory birds stop there for a moment. Frogs, toads

and lizards have all come back and the other day I even found a salamander.

"Here they enjoy perfect freedom. We hardly disturb them at all and they can nest without fear and find all they need in the way of food."

Our host showed us the collection of photographs he had taken of the many species of trees in flower. "Look," he said as he showed us one of the photographs, "I caught a spider eating a greenfly, amazing isn't it?"

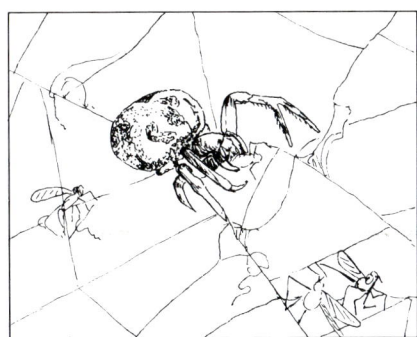

HOW TO BUILD YOUR VERY OWN CITY NATURE RESERVE.

It was a wonderful surprise to see the variety and diversity of nature on that little patch of forsaken land.

I went back home convinced that anything was possible. They had started with less than most city gardeners. Our gardens are actually a collection of nature reserves that must not disappear.

Each of us has the essential tool: a small garden. We can preserve and improve both plant and animal life, even in the middle of a large urban area.

If you take on this commitment it will be hard work. But it will be worthwhile, for each year you will find that your garden will give you new pleasures and rewards.

Before you begin.

You must first think about the trees and shrubs you are going to plant, for these tend to take longer to grow. Above all, do not rush into anything. It's always best to plan before you buy anything. So read and take time to sit in your garden assessing the advantages that are already there. Above all *don't* start by clearing out anything, except the rubbish – yet!

Take your time. Go carefully.

Plants which like shady conditions: Hortensia, scented willow, wild stawberry, fern, iris pseudacorus, goat's beard and star of Bethlehem.

Plants can adapt to the town.

Our town gardens are not always the most ideal places for plants. But nature is often very adaptable and plants can be grown almost anywhere. You don't really need to be an expert to grow plants. You just need a little enthusiasm and a few simple guidelines.

Many town gardens already have a good basis on which to build. Improve your garden around the existing layout and you won't find it too difficult. Overgrown grass and old herbaceous borders are wonderful for butterflies, birds and wildlife in general.

Other gardens, though, will be neglected, cemented, dumping grounds. If you are the owner of one of these "gardens" you will have to use your imagination in

Specialist nurseries and botanical gardens.

It's probably a good idea to visit a good garden supplier or a botanical garden. Botanical gardens are excellent sources of inspiration! They will give you the opportunity to look at shrubs, bushes and trees enabling you to make more informed choices. Above all, it will help diversify your selection by introducing you to plants previously unknown to you. Make a note of both the common and Latin name for the plants you choose so that you don't risk getting a different plant from the one you wanted.

During your visit to the gardens, find out where you can get the various shrubs and plants and which are the most suitable varieties for you and the conditions in your particular garden.

Exchanging plants with your friends.

It's fun to discuss your plans for your garden with friends who share your love of nature and who have already established their garden.

It doesn't cost anything to exchange cuttings and plants. You'll also have a tale to tell when friends ask you where you acquired them. Gardening enthusiasts hate to waste unwanted cuttings or plants just because they have nowhere to plant them. You'll be doing them a good turn.

Why don't you and your friends organize a system whereby you swap plants and shrubs? These plants are often smaller at the beginning, but they soon grow strong and are often better adapted to their environment.

order to make it a beautiful natural habitat again. It will certainly be worthwhile once you see the return of the extraordinary variety of life forms.

HOW TO USE THIS BOOK.

The purpose of this book is to provide encouragement in the task of "furnishing" your garden – with the same care as you would if you were decorating the interior of your house. I hope this book will provide simple guidelines to follow which will help you to succeed. I have placed the emphasis on characteristics typical of town gardens. The practical tips you pick up from this book will enable you to get immediate and satisfying results which will encourage you to persevere with the task in hand.

My intention has been to help you to broaden your choice and to look at the different options open to you so that you can introduce into your garden the widest variety of trees and shrubs available to you. I hope this will provide you with the greatest scope possible when selecting your plants, which is, anyway, essential for good ecological balance.

Less well known species suggested in this book have been chosen on account of their rarity and their beneficial effects on our

environment. You will not find the names of some of the most common trees and shrubs, like the lilac or the forsythia, but this is no good reason for discounting them altogether!

Keep what's there and work around it ...

"Sunlight and the Layout of Your Garden".

This chapter will give you tips on the different characteristics of town gardens. These will help you to choose the basic plants and shrubs you wish to grow in your shape of garden and with the amount of sunlight that reaches your garden. You may also want to improve the soil to help your plants grow.

The later chapters of the book will cover particular subjects in greater detail: trees, flowers, patios, ponds, climbing plants, rock plants and hedges.

Suggestions are designed according to your degree of interest in gardening.

All advice is given under three recurring headings below. Spot yourself before you begin.

"For the enthusiast": those who just love gardening! They are prepared to make sacrifices in all weathers. They would be able to grow a plant in a glass of water in the depths of the cellar. They are fascinated by all aspects of nature, very knowledgeable and are never short of ideas. No challenge is more fascinating than a gardening problem and they use whatever space is available to them to grow something new. In short, they are always ready to try anything.

"For the idle gardener": those who love their garden but have little time to devote to it – for those who prefer to read among the foliage rather than set to work. However, there's nothing to prevent them from establishing once and for all a good garden foundation plan that will need little attention but that will be pleasing to the eye throughout the year.

"For the occasional gardener": those who prefer results to hard graft! They are "fair-weather" gardeners, who from time to time feel the urge to put on their gardening

gloves, and dash out to plant rows of seeds. They simply have very little free time and usually don't see the results of their moments of enthusiasm. Others feel very helpless when they come across plant problems.

The book contains twenty pages of tables divided into simple categories to help you to select unusual species of plants.

These tables were designed to help you choose from the various species on offer and make interesting combinations of flora.

The species have been put into categories according to their most relevant characteristics for a town garden: height of an adult plant; adaptability to shady conditions, shape etc.

Three garden layouts.

Three layouts have been made up by a landscape architect. You will find ways to get around problems typical of many town gardens: size, shape, existing plants, lack of sunlight etc.

We have laid these out in the form of diagrams with code numbers for the different species. We only tell you the most significant characteristics and conditions required of the plants you wish to choose. You can then select the most suitable plants and combinations for your garden from the model layouts in this book.

SUNLIGHT.

The majority of town gardens are set out in the form of squares with buildings on each side. These enclosed patches of land vary in size, the largest measuring about half a hectare. These patches of land are divided into several small private gardens which are often of a rectangular shape. The width of the garden is the same as the width of the house and the length varies from between 20-60ft (7-20m). The position of the garden will determine the amount of sunlight it receives and the type of plants you can grow in it.

Town gardens often have terraces of varying sizes leading to the house. Many houses also have flat roof terraces which have been or can be converted into raised roof gardens.

Over the years, many gardens have been built on with garages, sheds and extensions.

In some areas, tall skyscrapers have replaced houses which means that many gardens are now completely shaded from the sun. Sometimes only one or two tiny gardens exist, hemmed in by all sorts of buildings.

These are all factors which may affect the sun in your garden as well as the distance separating it from buildings opposite. The layout of its walls in relation to the

sun in summer and in winter, when it is lower in the sky, also affects your garden. You must also take into account shade from trees which varies depending on whether the trees are deciduous or evergreen.

If your immediate surroundings are covered in deciduous trees, which lose their leaves in winter, your garden will have more light in winter and early spring. In the summer, trees blocking the path of the sun will mean that your garden is covered in shade for hours on end. (Fig. 1)

However, whatever the aspect and position of your garden, it is

fig 1

rare for a garden not to receive at least a few hours sun a day. The number of hours will vary according to the time of year.

Which way does your garden face?

In winter, when the sun is low over the horizon, the part facing south will receive more sun than the rest. The rays of sun, weaker during this time of year, will throw the shadow from the house away from the garden. North-facing gardens receive the least light. (Fig. 2)

In summer, all gardens are exposed to the sun at some point. In the morning, those facing east will be warmed by the sun. At midday, the light is beamed down almost vertically and most areas will receive it. The afternoon is better for those gardens facing west. (Fig. 3)

You will see that first one wall of your garden is covered in sun, and then the other. Only the north-facing wall will receive no direct sunlight. During the summer, when the sun is at its strongest, this part will benefit from indirect sunlight. (Fig. 4)

You will need quite a long time just looking at your garden throughout the four seasons so that you can really get to know the amount of sunlight each part of your garden receives. It's a good idea to make a few notes so that you can use the space available to its best advantage. If you are in a real hurry to start work, have a look at the sunrise and sunset in your garden. With a little imagination you will be able to

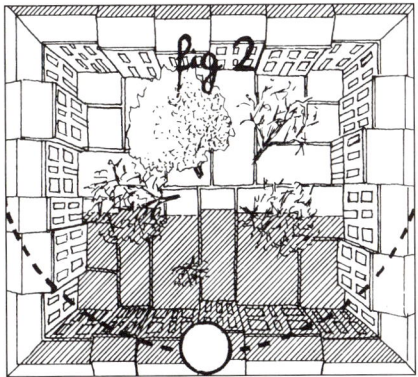

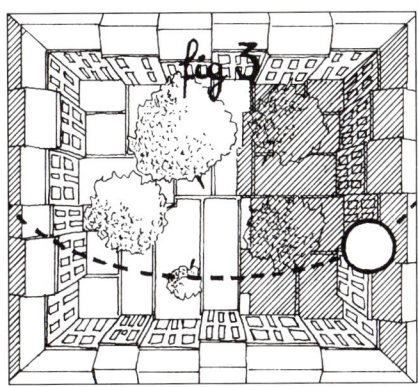

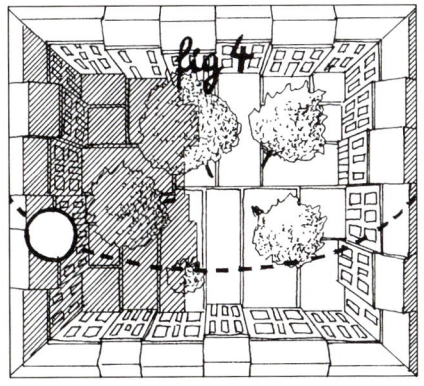

make a valid assessment of the light in your garden throughout the seasons.

To help you to do this, first take a look at the example of a southeast facing garden which receives plenty of sun. (Fig. 5, below.)

In the morning, triangle ABC is sunny.

At midday, during the summer, the whole garden is sunny. In the winter, the bottom of the garden is in the shade.

In the afternoon, triangles DAB and ABC are exposed to the sun until it disappears behind the houses.

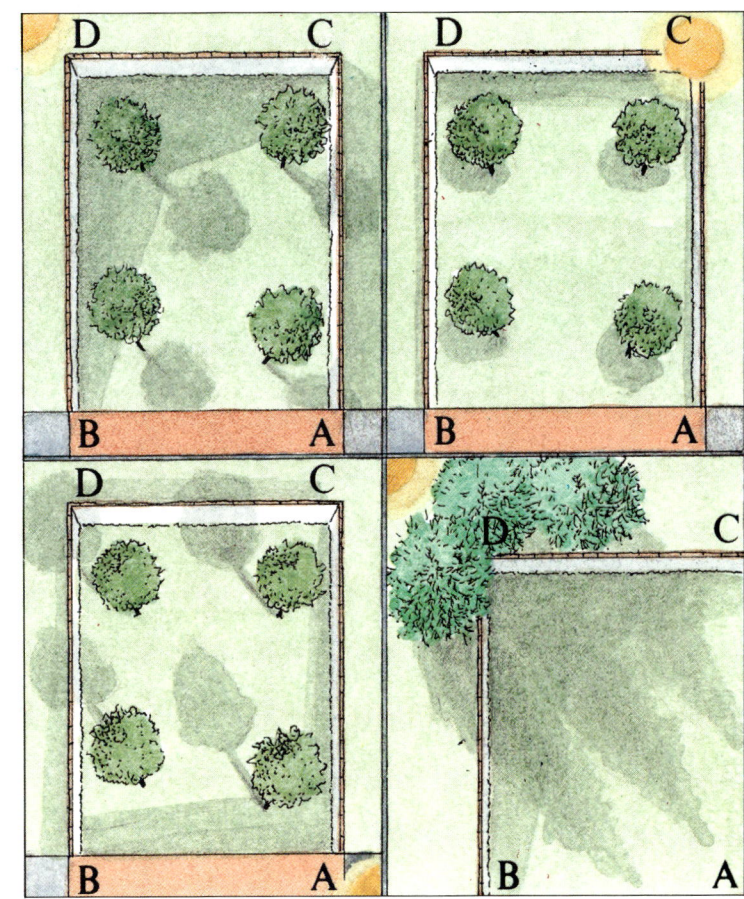

It is wall DB, therefore, which is most exposed to the sun. However, anything blocking the path of the sun will prevent it from shining on your garden.

You must not underestimate the benefits which can result from slight shade coming through the trees during the summer: it does more good than harm.

If you have established that your garden receives very little sun, either because it faces north or because there are too many tall buildings and trees blocking the sun at certain times of the day, do not despair. There are many plants which do not like the sun and enjoy the shade. Your garden may be shadier, but it is also more magical.

Raised balconies tend to get more sunlight because there are fewer obstacles blocking it.

POOR SOIL: WHAT YOU CAN DO.

I am not about to give you a lesson on the scientific make-up of soil, but there are certain things you should know about it. I will give you a few simple hints as to how you can improve it and so get the best out of your garden and plants.

As a general rule town soil tends to be very acidic. The main causes of this are shade, dampness and rain.

Whether soil is light or heavy, it is most probably lacking in organic matter. The soil is often not well-covered enough and is not helped at all by being exposed to the elements. It becomes crusty and very little will grow. The things you have planted will be stunted and will die off completely in the winter.

Most flowering and most forest species are able to grow in an acid soil, but you must still reduce the level of acidity in your garden. You can do this by sprinkling lime regularly, at least around the area where you have planted things.

SOME EXAMPLES OF DIFFERENT TYPES OF GARDENS.

A. The garden is quite sunny. There are several medium-sized trees and a few shrubs at the bottom of it with a clear space near the front. (Fig. 6)

Under the trees the soil will be richer on account of the humus made up of dead leaves. The surface of this soil is lightweight and dark; underneath it is paler, more compact and moist.

In the clear space near the front of the garden the soil is often lighter in weight and sandier in texture. It tends to dry out very quickly after it has rained. Its surface forms a dry crust and plants find it difficult to grow. The few plants which do will probably be rather scraggy and unhealthy. The soil is richer at the back of the garden than it is in the front.

The combination in this garden means that the soil is too acidic.

At the bottom of the garden it is sufficient to use some hydrated lime or ground limestone which

doesn't wash through the soil so quickly. This is particularly important during the first few years when you should use this at least once a year, in August or September. After the soil has improved noticeably, use it about once every two or three years.

At the front of the garden you must introduce some organic matter into the soil in the spring. Concentrate mostly on the areas which you intend to cultivate. You can use compost, properly decomposed manure, or peat with organic fertilizer added to it.

B. Your garden only receives a little sun and what's more it is full of plants. The soil is moist and mossy. Water starts to stagnate after it has rained and no grass will grow. (Fig. 7)

Your soil is acidic and very wet. You must treat it regularly with natural lime in order to redress the balance if you wish to introduce plants that are not happy in acid soil. You can use, of course, some manure or peat to make the soil a little lighter.

You would be wise to choose vigorous plants suitable for shady conditions and acid soil. To help them grow, you can use compost suitable for this type of plant.

If, however, you have a small area in your garden which has plenty of air and sun, you can im-

prove the soil in this area by following the instructions given in "A". Here you can plant species of plants that are hard to please.

You could even build a pond surrounded by a variety of plants that are happy in swampy conditions. This would be pretty and highly original.

C. Your garden receives a lot of sunlight and there are hardly any trees. It is neglected and full of weeds. (Fig. 8)

The areas in which you intend to put in plants must be thoroughly turned over with a spade. As you dig, the grass on the surface may be broken up and mixed with the soil at the bottom of the trench. You are now ready to follow the instructions in "A".

D. Your garden is empty and gets very little sun. The soil has subsided, having been trodden on frequently, and is completely bare.

You must dig up and turn over the soil as in "C". If your soil is heavy and sticky you must add decomposed manure or compost. As in previous examples, you must treat the soil with lime in early winter. Shortage of sunshine means that you should also use more fertilizer and lime on this type of soil especially if you want to grow more difficult plants. Hardy (frost-tolerant) varieties are better than others in this case.

E. The garden is well looked after, but things do not grow well in it. Plants dry out in the summer and die in the winter. Trees don't seem to grow very much and do not bear fruit. The rose bushes are diseased.

In the spring thoroughly treat the area around the trees with well-rotted manure. You can also treat plants in the same way, or you can dig them up in early winter, turn over the soil treating it with organic fertilizer or compost and then put the plants back in their place.

In early winter you must also sprinkle lime on the surface and repeat this treatment for the following two or three years until the plants show vigorous growth.

A good short-cut for the lazy.

If you dread carrying out major tasks in your garden, you can still improve the soil in your garden by using a fork in the area around shrubs and trees. In the spring you can add compost or organic fertilizer and simply dig this in to the earth with a fork.

You will still need to sprinkle some lime on the soil in the first days of winter. (You'll need to use between ¼-½lb per sq.yd or 80-100g per sq.m).

When you plant shrubs, you must dig a hole big enough to easily accommodate all the roots. Feed the soil at the bottom of the hole before putting in your plant. In the following spring don't forget to treat the soil around the plants with organic fertilizer or compost.

By following this method for several years running, you will find that the soil around the plants has improved and that the plants themselves look greener, healthier and stronger. They will also start to flower better.

Lime must not be mixed with other soil dressings, so to avoid the loss of plant foods, you must allow a certain amount of time between sprinkling the lime and treating the soil with compost or organic fertilizer. That is why we have suggested here that you use the lime in early winter and add the compost or organic fertilizer in the spring.

Fertilizer, manure, compost, lime.

You can see from the previous examples that it is essential to introduce new nutrients into your garden.

There are many different types of fertilizers on the market. When you use them, be sure to follow the instructions on the packet.

If you decide to improve your soil in this way, only select natural fertilizers so that you don't damage the environment. Try to find dried manure, guano, dried blood, bonemeal, seaweed etc., which are all perfectly safe to use.

My compost heap.

In the north-facing part of the garden in a shady area, which is good for decomposition, I have assembled four wooden fences (old pallets for transporting goods will do). The front of this container is detachable to make it easier to empty it out. I have used preservative on the wood to protect it. At the bottom of the container I have made a slight hollow in the ground (about 6in (15cm) deep). This hollow helps to hold in the moisture which aids decomposition.

I throw all sorts of things on to the compost heap, including grass cuttings, leaves, twigs, small branches (break these up into pieces no longer than 4in (10cm)), dead leaves, withered flowers, old soil from flowerpots and so on. You can use anything natural and not man-made.

I also use bio-degradable household waste, such as old vegetables, vegetable peelings, meals left on the plate, fishbones, crushed eggshells (this is lime), coffee grounds, tea bags, ashes from the log fire, even chicken and meat bones. Don't worry, you won't produce a terrible smell. Just make sure that the layers forming naturally on the compost heap are levelled out and they will break down and decompose.

As I don't need to add lime to my soil, I empty this container, with a fork, at the end of the summer. The top layer is still not properly decomposed, so I will save that and put it at the bottom of the container when I have finished the job. The rest is dark and the lumps of compost can be easily broken up. The texture is still quite coarse: you will notice the odd chicken bone or piece of eggshell. They won't spoil the beauty of your garden and will be appreciated by certain birds. These particles will continue to decompose in the ground and will make the soil softer and much more permeable.

With the help of a basket, I spread the compost around the plants, covering the soil with a fairly thin layer (1in (2-3cm)). The compost will continue to decompose throughout the winter and will protect the roots of the plants from very bitter frosts.

In the spring I just turn over the soil around the plants with a fork.

This mixes the compost in with the topsoil.

After two or three years of this simple treatment, the appearance of your garden will be transformed. Plants will be greener and will grow more vigorously. The soil will become softer and will retain the right amount of moisture. You won't have to sprinkle lime nearly so frequently to reduce the acidity of cultivated soil.

In certain cases I still use a little manure to help fruit-bearing trees and bushes. I use manure around the raspberry bushes and vines along the garden walls as well as around the rose bushes to help them to grow.

I regularly use lime on my lawn which is too acid and to help revive the compost in my flower pots which seems to go acid quickly.

For azaleas, rhododendrons, conifers and evergreen plants, like camelias or lemon trees, I always use a special ericaceous compost. These species do not tolerate lime in the soil and thrive in acid soil rich in organic matter.

I have completely given up trying to grow vegetables in my garden. They seem to need a lot of sun and do not like the exceptionally high acidity levels and the shadows cast by the trees. The only exception to this is cress which grows anywhere.

I have, however, made room for herbs in the sunny borders of my garden. They smell nice, have pretty flowers and only need a little attention.

Lime.

You will find a variety of lime products on the market, but hydrated lime is the best. Again, it's always wise to follow the instructions on the packet regarding the correct quantities to use. Just sprinkle the lime on to the surface of the soil and lightly dig it in with a fork. On the lawn, I use a water sprinkler to help the lime penetrate deep into the soil.

ESTABLISHING A PLAN FOR YOUR GARDEN.

Build around what you already have.

When you decide to add to or make a plan for your garden using new species of plants, it is wise to bear in mind the plants already in your garden so that all the plants and trees will complement each other and give you the best possible variety of sizes and shades of leaves and flowers. Think about how you are going to arrange the species throughout the seasons and about having a few evergreens and some winter-flowering plants to add a little green to your garden during the winter months.

Your garden is not empty.

If the existing plants are very old, they are probably very interesting. So try to work around the plants you already have rather than dig them up.

If the plants in your garden have been put in recently, they may have been put there without much thought: trees blocking the sun in the best part of the day or in an

inconvenient position; a plant which is there without apparent rhyme or reason.

It is for you to decide what to keep and what to get rid of. Keep them if you can. The plants already there may inspire you and help you to build the garden of your dreams around them.

In certain cases, you can move a species to another place. You

can only do this with young plants less than three years old and you should move them between November and March.

You can also prune a tree into the form of a bush. I have done just that with a pyracantha and it now takes up much less space in my garden and has enabled me to grow a peach tree next to it. Likewise, a hornbeam has taken root at the foot of the old pear tree and I have been able to prune it to give the effect of an informal tree-lined path. The result is rather attractive and original.

A basic principle is that it's better to put up with little inconveniences than to pull out plants that have been there for years.

Your choices.

You must first decide which trees you would like to have in your garden. If you decide to have a very large tree in your garden or if there is one there already, the whole of the garden must be worked around it. Nothing can replace the value to wildlife of a really large tree. Over five hundred baby trees do not support as much wildlife as one two-hundred-year-old oak tree.

If your garden is small you could put seats around the trunk of the tree.

If your garden is larger than 18 sq.yd (15 sq.m) you could fill up the bottom of the garden with

trees and leave a more open space at the front.

In both cases certain smaller trees and shrubs may be planted. (See the chapter on "Trees".)

Open space.

It's important that you don't turn your garden into a forest by planting trees everywhere. You should keep an open space to allow the sunlight in 30-40 sq.ft (3-4 sq.m). This space, even if it's only small, will give an impression of depth in your garden. It will also provide good conditions for a much wider variety of insect and bird species.

If you have enough sunlight in your garden you can grow a lawn. If there's a lot of shade it's probably best to cover this space with natural gravel and stones (for a better effect, they should be uneven in size) or old paving stones leaving large gaps between them. It doesn't take much to look after them and the effect will be quite original. Light and heat will reflect better off them.

Solid concrete is not only ugly but means death to all plant and insect species.

Flower-beds.

Make a space for your flower-beds along the walls most exposed to the sun. They should be at least 2 ft 6 in (80 cm) wide and

here you will be able to plant species varying in height depending on their position in the flower-bed. It's important that you take into consideration the size of the plants. By mixing medium-sized trees, shrubs, and large and small plants, you will find that this will give your garden greater depth and texture.

A flower-bed 3 ft (1m) wide and 40 ft (12m) long can easily accommodate about a hundred different species: one or two trees, three or four large shrubs, one or two climbing plants, three or four small shrubs broken up by a great variety of hardy flowers of differing

sizes. You can also use rock plants and summer bedding plants along the borders.

Long gardens.

If your garden is twice as long as it is wide it is better to break up the straight lines by having a roundish flower-bed at the front or back of the garden.

If your garden is three times as long as it is wide you can try to disguise the length of it by putting in clusters of greenery such as a low medlar tree, an unpruned privet and a series of hazel bushes. You can use this as a quiet area surrounded by greenery. Remember that you can plant more in the bottom third of the garden as well as building a pond in the sunniest part.

Hedges and walls.

If your garden is surrounded by a hedge, let it grow freely rather than cut it into a square shape. If you plant your own hedge, vary it by using different species. You'll be pleasantly surprised by the results. It will be very pretty and will attract many birds, butterflies and insects. They give good cover to hedgehogs, shrews and other small creatures.

Your garden walls should not be bare. Try to hide them under the greenery. Where you don't have any trees or bushes, or even behind these, put in climbing

plants to cover the garden wall and the wall of the house. It's lovely in the summer and you may find you attract some rather useful little animals.

Plants grow bigger.

When you decide to put in your plants remember that young

plants get bigger. Make sure you leave enough space for each variety, even if it looks rather bare at the beginning. For the time being, you can fill these spaces with hardy plants which you can easily remove when necessary.

A garden with enough different varieties and species is in a state of perpetual change. There is always room for improvement and you can make little changes here and there.

My suggestions for the idle gardener.

Don't worry too much about working out the amount of sun your garden gets. Just plant a pretty, decorative tree of a vigorous variety in a good position and surround it with bushes.

Once winter has arrived, leave the dead leaves to decompose. In the spring turn over the soil around the trees and shrubs using a fork. Feed your trees with a little dried manure from a packet. This will help them to grow vigorously.

Cover the middle of your garden with irregular paving stones. You should lay them down on wet soil without cement. Moss will start growing in between them. You can also grow pearlwort which, like common moss to which it is related, grows well in damp conditions and produces pretty white flowers.

For the occasional gardener.

Look at the trees already in your garden and work around them. It won't be long before you get attractive results. Surround them with flowering or fruit-bearing shrubs or evergreens of differing sizes and shapes. Use easy-to-grow climbing plants such as ivy, vine, climbing or rambling roses, honeysuckle and sweet peas.

Your compost heap will be very simple. Pile up twigs in a damp part of the garden between the shrubs and bushes and add to it any scraps you have. You may even attract a little wren.

Turn your garden lawn into a meadow by adding flowering clover seed to your ordinary grass seed and planting a few crocuses in the first year.

For the enthusiast.

Take note of the amount of sunshine on each of your flower-beds. This will give you a better idea what to plant in the shade and what in the sun.

If you have enough space make a double compost container. You'll find you'll fill up the second as soon as the first one is full of decomposed compost. You can use this whenever you need to fill up a trough or put in some plants.

Make sure you have enough space for climbing plants. Break up the lines in your garden with different clusters of plants and by using different shapes in your flower-beds. Put flowering plants in beds at the foot of the largest trees. Establish rock gardens in sunny

parts of the garden. Mix old-fashioned rose bushes with hardy flowering plants. Find out which are the best plants for the shadier areas in your garden.

My tips.

I always keep a bag of peat in my cellar. It's useful for making the soil more acid in areas where I grow heather. I add it to the compost for flower pots, house plants and seed trays. I use it carefully because the peat bogs are being dug out.

In the summer when I water the garden I also water the compost heap. This accelerates the decomposition process.

I replace old trees by putting in a young tree of my choice nearby.

For the path leading to the lawn I have used old hexagonal paving stones set out in a Japanese-style path.

TREES

TREES ARE ESSENTIAL.

Trees and shrubs are an essential part of our little gardens. Their growth contributes to our forever changing landscape. Our own trees, intermingled with those of nearby gardens, provide us with a whole range of different shades of green, that change with each season.

It is in spring when we are most aware of the ephemeral beauty of their blossom and the gentle greens of their new foliage.

When the summer comes round again, our town gardens surrounded by high walls are just like greenhouses. The plants which are too exposed to the burning sun are scraggy and tend not to grow well. The soil dries up and becomes poor. The gentle shade of the trees is necessary to keep it cool.

Lastly, trees and bushes add a graceful, magical element to our gardens.

There are many different species of trees which are perfect for our climate. So don't be afraid to vary and build on the selection we offer you, for each species has its own special function. The more types you have, the greater the number and variety of insects you will attract. These will protect your plants from greenfly and other harmful pests. They will also help

with the process of pollination, so producing a good crop of fruit. Indigenous species – those that are native to the country – are the most supportive of local insect and bird species. Foreign, exotic trees and plants are the natural food for foreign animal species. So choose indigenous species whenever possible.

Trees and insects will attract a great variety of birds which come into our garden to find shelter, food and somewhere to fly around. And the greater the variety of trees in an area, the more support they give to the wildlife.

Trees are essential for the preservation of nature, even in the heart of a big city. One great oak can support over four hundred

different species of animals and insects.

We should follow in the footsteps of our ancestors by having fruit trees in our gardens – a delight to us as well as to our feathered friends. Wild or cultivated fruit has a very special taste and we can rediscover a host of long-forgotten, but delicious fruits, for use in recipes from our grandmothers' time...

There are still trees in our town gardens.

People who had houses built more than a hundred years ago worked in close collaboration with nature. They would carefully negotiate the purchase of a few square feet of land which for them was to be a refuge from the ever-increasing development and noise of the city.

We can see by the vast number of fruit trees in our older gardens that our ancestors wanted to be able to eat home-grown fruit. They planted many different types of espaliers, such as peach and cherry, bearing a good crop of fruit. Sometimes you see remains of currant and raspberry bushes.

They combined usefulness with beauty and they mixed pretty fruit trees with majestic lime trees, the freshness of red or green hazel trees with the heavy scent of lilac. They planted acacias, wisterias and apple trees alongside red or pink hawthorns, providing shelter for hedgerow birds.

They compensated for the bareness of winter by planting holly, yew trees, juniper or box-wood – foodstores for hedgerow birds. Ivy was used for the front of houses and garden walls.

Remains of a garden or return to the forest?

Wherever you look our small gardens are full of old sycamore, ash or chestnut trees.

Nature seems to have taken over from the early occupants who long since died of old age.

When you see a huge tree in the small garden you have just inherited, you probably want to chop it down, since you dream of having a vegetable garden.

I suggest you don't buy the home unless you are truly in love with the large tree whose overbearing presence makes you feel that you are in the middle of a dense forest.

Over the years the birds have taken over the place. If you get rid of this natural shelter, the sudden disturbance could cause them irreparable damage.

If you're not a keen gardener, why not find an empty garden. There are many of them about that have already received shock treatment and have been turned into sun terraces. Gardens with trees that need protection need keen garden-lovers.

It takes decades for a tree to mature, but the advantages of having them certainly outweigh the disadvantages.

Don't chop them down!

You mustn't take this to the extreme by allowing little seedlings planted by the wind to grow all over your garden each spring.

If the garden you have just inherited has been neglected for some years there's a good chance that local woodland plants have taken root. That's how you find different types of seedlings in the most unexpected of places.

If you want to, keep one or two which are in the best position but thin out the others if they are very

small and overcrowded.

You should remove sycamores without delay, replacing them with more suitable species. Our town

gardens must be cultivated with restraint and we must be careful not to turn them into dark forests of sycamore trees! [1] Conservation volunteers spend a lot of time trying to clear forests of these invaders.

How to look after these old trees.

An electric chain saw is cheap and often rather too easy to use. Some people think that they can become veteran tree surgeons overnight! It is not unknown for beautiful trees to be damaged permanently or even killed by people whose original aim was just to prune them.

1. *You cannot chop down any tree that has a preservation order on it, without first consulting your local authority.*

There are other so-called advantages in using this destructive method: you might get a few minutes more sun in the summer; you won't have so many leaves to rake up in the winter. It's just not worth it, for it will take years for an old tree to regain its past glory – that's if it doesn't die!

An adult tree, whether it be a forest tree or merely ornamental, doesn't need you to help it. There is nothing more beautiful than the natural position and growth of its branches. Remove only the dead branches, and to be sure of making no mistake, you are better to do this in the summer months.

If certain low branches are causing an obstruction or bother you too much, you can take off a few lower branches. Whatever you do, don't touch the main branches which give the tree its shape. And always, but always, leave a "cuff" or stump when you take off even a small branch. If you cut too close to the main trunk you can damage

or even kill the main tree. The cadmium layer just under the bark is the growing point of a tree so avoid damage to this at all costs.

Standard fruit trees more than three years old do not require very much attention. Simply prune the dead wood and the intertwining branches.

Severe pruning of a fruit tree by cutting off its main branches can have devastating results and can completely ruin the appearance of the tree. You can cut the branches very short, but it's a very complicated job and best done by an experienced gardener. If your tree is old, keep it looking beautiful rather than worrying about how much fruit it produces. You may even be able to plant a small replacement tree near it.

We have not yet discussed the case of fruit trees which were originally grown as espaliers but because of years of neglect have become ordinary trees, or indeed that of fruit trees intended to be ornamental trees growing too close to a party wall.

The best solution is to come to an arrangement with the people next door so that you both look after and protect the tree. If you can do this, then there are two possibilities:

Leave the tree free to grow as it pleases and do nothing more than look at it.

If it is an espalier fruit tree, prune it properly into a tall upright tree. This produces superb results and a lot of fruit, although you do need to know what you are doing and you have to be prepared to spend some time on it each year.

If neither party is enthusiastic about its height and want to cut it down to the level of the party wall, do call in an expert tree surgeon to do it for you.

BUSHES AND SHRUBS THAT HAVE SURVIVED.

Sometimes we may find that we have discovered certain special species of bushes and shrubs. In addition to their beauty they are also vital for the ecological balance in our gardens. The most common are the many different shades of lilac bushes and the many different species of wisteria. Others include: traditional un-pruned boxwood which forms pretty evergreen bushes; spiraea which has clusters of small white flowers in the month of May; meadow viburnum and scented syringa with small white flowers;

A small garden full of sweet-smelling bushes: lilac, boxwood, spiraea, old-fashioned climbing rose. What a delight for local birds and insects!

climbing rose-bushes with their old-fashioned scents.

All these bushes and shrubs play an important part, for they add to the diversity of plant life. Some of them are rich in pollen and attract and provide nourishment for essential insects, such as the bee, and butterflies. Low bushes are used as hiding places by certain hedgerow birds like the wren. And they're vital in suburban gardens for the survival of hedgehogs.

For the lazy gardener, bushes are a gift. They smother weeds. Planting ground cover plants plus a few new bushes where the old ones have died is all you need to do. Some bushes, like rosemary, (which is dearly loved by bees) do have a limited life-span, and will need to be replaced.

Adding extra bushes with silver or red foliage can add life to an existing dull clump of bushes. The buddleia is a shrub with exceptional value to butterflies, bees and insects. It shoots rapidly and can be cut back strongly at the end of each summer. It's wonderful to help you make a standing start or to revitalize a tired patch.

Like trees, bushes give your garden texture and depth as well as a little mystery. Rather than cut them down hastily, we must care for them in the same way as we do for our trees.

Let's rebuild our garden around existing trees and shrubs.

What do we do with the little, old garden we have just inherited?

Let us first go up to the top of the house and look at our small plot of land, probably part of a larger area divided into a grid by walls overflowing with a variety of vegetation. You will get a general impression as to the character of the garden: meadow, ornamental

or woodland. These are the first things to look for.

Let's try to develop the garden in keeping with the whole of the surrounding area. It will help guarantee success.

To improve this little nature reserve even more we shall make some unusual choices of plants that have adapted well to the conditions in this country.

Fruit trees are happy in town gardens. You can introduce any kind of fruit trees and bushes to

your garden, including vines and apricot trees, for the warmer micro-climate of the town garden makes it possible for them to produce a good crop.

When making your selection, choose more unusual species that are not already in your garden, or those species that are already over a hundred years old. You can also introduce into your garden wild ornamental fruit trees and bushes, like the crab apple, plum, wild cherry and the different varieties of elder.

Don't put similar species near each other. If you have a superb pine tree in your garden, don't then plant a Christmas tree in it as well. It does not adapt well to the town, will take up all your spare space and be completely superfluous.

Lime trees are magnificent,

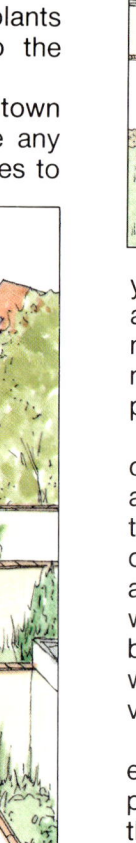

scented trees and their pollen attracts numerous insects. Lime trees can live for more than one thousand years and can grow to a huge size. If you are tempted to plant one, first take account of the amount of your garden it will occupy as it gets bigger. You must put it in the most central position possible in your garden, being sure you leave a polite space between it and your party walls.

If conditions are not absolutely right or if there is already a lime tree nearby, it's best to plant something else yourself. It's advisable to do this so that you have a greater variety of large trees such as oak, beech, walnut or even a standard cherry tree.

This rule does not have to be followed so rigidly when it comes to medium-sized trees as there are so many different types. Examples of these are fruit trees, such as apple, pear, plum and peach, as well as ornamental trees, like mountain ash, hawthorn and hazel.

Your golden rule should be to vary the trees as much as possible by planting different species or, at the very least, different varieties of the same species.

When you plant fruit trees you must take into account the way each one of them pollinates. Certain types of tree need to be close to another tree of the same species that blossoms at the same time. The introduction of

certain pollinating varieties can improve the overall crop of your trees. Your nursery will advise you about all the different possible combinations.

Several varieties of apple tree belonging to old species have reappeared in the nurseries. It's best to choose these as they need very little attention and produce a good quantity of fruit. They have a very different taste from most apples on the market and are quite a pleasant discovery.

Do take my word for it, these standard apple trees with their pink blossoms are one of the prettiest sights of spring.

All sorts of other trees, which have not been around for years, can be brought back into our town garden: the silver birch adored by blue tits and hedge sparrows; the black or white mulberry tree; the hazel, the medlar, the whitebeam, juniper and yew. These trees can become a part of our everyday surroundings and are much less demanding than fruit trees.

Again, remember that native trees support native wildlife. Imported varieties do not support wildlife. And many quite common trees are not native.

In gardens where there's a lot of shade the hardier, more vigorous varieties are better. It's advisable to plant compact varieties of conifers or those with a high crown so that they don't take up too much space in your small

garden. There are also cultivated species which are more slender and take up little space. Bear in mind that many conifers are foreign and support little wildlife. You should have a much smaller number of conifers than other types of trees. A proportion of one in twenty is quite sufficient.

Let's plant some trees!

When you plant a tree remember that it will grow at its own pace.

Imagine an adult tree in the place you've chosen for it and make sure that it doesn't block out the sun too much. Then imagine what effect it will have for the people who live next door.

In a small garden measuring 20 x 50ft (6 x 15m) don't have more than two trees measuring over 20ft (6m) high. Only have one, if it's a really large tree, like a walnut or standard cherry. Rather than planting it in the corner or at the bottom of the garden, put it in the middle.

You can put smaller trees, bushes and shrubs around the larger trees. These will encourage a tall tree to reach for the light and to grow rapidly. These bushes can then be taken out or will die as the main tree gains maturity.

The distance between large trees should be about 20ft (7m), but smaller species can be planted closer to one another. Silver birches can be planted in twos or threes, about 6ft (2m) apart. Always bear in mind the adult size of these "filler" trees and their capacity to adapt to the increasing shade produced by taller trees.

The distance between smaller trees can vary between 5ft (1.5m) and 10-12ft (3-4m). A distance of 5-8ft (1.5-2.5m) is appropriate between bushes and shrubs.

For example, you can plant a peach tree against a wall that is very exposed to the sun 6ft (2m) away from a birch, a laburnum or other species with delicate foliage. You can still plant bushes such as raspberry, gooseberry or currant in front of it, and you can put in some wild strawberry plants underneath. By planting in this way, you will make the best use of the space available.

So long as you keep to the distances necessary between trees you can, if you want, have a garden full of different species, alternating fruit trees with other types, as well as trees of differing heights, blossom times and brilliance of flowers.

Many people in this country are frightened of growing trees near the walls of their homes. The fears are largely groundless, as anyone who has visited a green city such as Washington will know. Again some people do not like the shade, but if you feel happy to look out into dappled light and cool greens, then don't hesitate to plant a tree just where you'd like it.

The incomparable charm of old-fashioned roses with a distinct ruffled appearance. Modern roses have been bred without the heavenly smell of the earlier varieties.

Let's put in lots of bushes.

There's still room for you to put in all sorts of bushes of your choice among the trees.

A tiny garden of your dreams, bursting with many different species of plants.

Those who like berries will plant bushes bearing edible fruits like redcurrants, raspberries, gooseberries, bilberries, blackberries, and blackcurrants. They are simple to maintain and are easily propagated either by taking cuttings or spontaneously by means of rhizomes as do raspberry bushes.

Save some room between bushes to plant hardy, herbal or ornamental plants. They'll add variety and beauty with the passing seasons.

The delightful prickly sloe bush with its white spring foliage and scores of little blue berries. Sloe is one of the best fruits for home-made wine. It's a perfect shelter for our sparrows.

It's worth mentioning the now-forgotten medlar tree – an old-fashioned species which could be described either as a large shrub or a small tree. If it's transplanted it can grow anywhere. Its pretty, white flowers and silver-green leaves will be a delight to you. It bears fruit, called medlars, rich in vitamin C and full of medicinal qualities.

Those with less time to devote to their garden will find a host of hardy, ornamental thorny shrubs and bushes from which to choose. Many reward you with blossoms and then berries, that last into the early winter months.

Don't worry about scratching yourself on the thorns from time to time because these plants are a great benefit to our feathered friends. You will be rewarded by the return of the little sparrows, whose well-sheltered nests you'll find in the spring months.

There are all sorts of lovely bushes which deserve a place in your garden including: sloes, hawthorns, and different varieties of perfumed shrubs or bush roses. Many of these are often used as ingredients for old-fashioned recipes and remedies.

When to buy your plants and put them in.

The best period is from November to March when the plants are dormant and when the ground is not frozen. This is the time when trees, too, shut down for the winter and will have time to adapt before the warmer months.

The only exception to this rule is when dealing with plants of the azalea and rhododendron families which are planted in acid soil in the spring. You must fill the hole with peat mixed with compost.

If you don't know the varieties of species, you will have to rely on gardening books. You can take these with you on a buying trip to the nursery. You should visit your nursery in the summer, especially if you want to pick up more unusual, old-fashioned varieties. You can see them in flower, but then you will probably have to put in a special order for them. And wait.

When the plant is delivered make sure that the one supplied is in good health: it should be vigorous and its bark should not be withered or covered with any suspicious spots. Its buds should be firm and shouldn't drop off when touched. The roots shouldn't be too short or damaged and should have been cut properly.

If you're not going to plant the trees or shrubs immediately, at least get them out of any hot or dry indoor surroundings. Put them outside, protected from the frost with the roots covered with light, damp soil. This waiting period shouldn't be more than a few days. And never let the roots dry out.

How are you going to plant them?

To plant your tree dig a hole measuring at least 20in (50cm) in all directions. While you are doing this soak the roots of your tree in

a bucket of water, to which you can add some rich garden soil. Fill the bottom of the hole with some organic topsoil. You can use manure as long as it's not in contact with the roots. This will help feed your plants in later years.

With enough room for the roots in the hole, the neck of your tree should be at surface level. If you received your tree or shrub in a pot, then plant exactly at the depth used by the nursery.

You can put back the rest of the soil around the tree keeping the stem well-positioned. When you have partially covered the roots, gently pack down the soil and give it a thorough first watering so that the whole thing stays together. Add the rest of the soil and pack it down again still holding the tree in an upright position.

Water it again thoroughly and finish with a mulch of rich leaf compost or decomposed manure. If you don't have this, just sprinkle on organic fertilizer and cover it with peat. But remember that this is the one and only time you'll have to feed your plant and to correct problems in the soil it will feed on. So take care whenever you plant.

In town gardens such as ours it is usually not necessary to use stakes. But if you do, drive the stake in before you refill the hole. Put the stake as close to the stem as possible, without damaging the roots, and use a tree tie to secure the tree to the stake.

What special care should you take?

The first year, be sure to water your tree during the summer. Limp leaves are a sign that it is thirsty. Don't hesitate to pour a whole bucket of water over the foot of the tree, being sure that the water is penetrating the soil properly.

It won't be necessary to prune your fruit trees the first year they are planted. Generally speaking, trees which have been bought from a nursery have usually already been pruned when you receive them. Get the nursery to tell you how to prune in the following two years, or alternatively, refer to the chapter in this book entitled "Pruning and Garden Maintenance".

After three years, when the crown of standard trees has been formed, they can do without pruning. The method of planting fruit trees using year-old scions, just sticks, is also worthwhile. This method of planting hardly needs any pruning. All you have to do is to make sure that the terminal bud receives all the nutrients it needs by shortening any shoot some 4in (10cm) from the central stem to a height of more or less 16in (40cm). These natural-shaped shrubs bear fruit very quickly.

If you want to make sure that you get a regular crop, it's best to prune espalier pear and apple trees and to clip the young shoots at the end of each spring. This method can also be used on currant bushes with excellent results.

Woody stems on raspberry bushes, where the fruit has grown, die and are replaced by new shoots. You must remove the dead wood after they have fruited and train the young shoots which are very pliable. In order to get a lot of fruit only leave three or four shoots at the foot of the raspberry bushes and space them 20in (50cm) apart.

In January it could be beneficial to use a cleaning spray made from a natural product on your fruit trees. This will reduce the likelihood of an invasion of harmful organisms or disease. It is best done when it is not frosty or windy, but it's not necessary to do this every year.

The most useful thing you can do for your trees is to feed them regularly with a rich compost, manure or natural fertilizer [2].

Choose carefully.

I have chosen trees and shrubs best acclimatized to our country or even plants more suited to a warmer climate, but which can also adapt to warmer town temperatures. I have divided them into three tables – and these follow at the end of this section.

_____

2. Refer to the chapter entitled "Pruning and Garden Maintenance".

Table I is for trees which are especially noted for their blossom and scent.

Table II groups together trees which are most noted for the beauty of their foliage at certain times of the year.

Table III offers a selection of species which are evergreen.

Each table is divided into three parts as follows:
Trees which prefer sunlight;
Trees which tolerate shade;
Trees which like the shade.

The most vigorous species, which adapt to all conditions, have been marked in green.

My suggestions for the idle gardener.

Gardening is not a passion of yours, but you do like gazing at nature. Plan your garden so that it looks attractive all year round, planting spring flowering plants, varied foliage for the summer and evergreens for the winter.

Make your selection as far as possible from the species marked in green in the tables as these are the easiest to look after.

Choose according to the amount of sunlight your garden receives and to the space available. Don't go for fruit trees as they need more care and attention. But if you like old-fashioned plants, choose from wild species such as the crab apple, plum, medlar and hazelnut.

First choose the tallest trees in the category which you find most attractive: flowering tree, ornamental or evergreen foliage. Then choose your shrubs from the second table. Complete your selection by choosing bushes from all three tables.

You can spread these plants out in all the space available as you won't need to leave room for flowers which need more regular attention.

Choose shrubs that tolerate shade or areas close to trees that are likely to grow tall. Put them in layered clumps to break up the length of the walls and fill out the corners.

An old house covered in greenery. A mature fruit tree and a number of shrubs and flowers. How lovely it is to see all the local birds enjoying themselves!

This garden with all its varied foliage will keep both you and the birds happy throughout the year.

For the occasional gardener.

You're not a born gardener but nevertheless you still like trying your hand at it. If you're not afraid to prune a shrub which is getting too big, why not add shrub roses to your selection? There are many lovely hardy varieties such as "Robusta" or "La Sevillana", which both flower over a very long period, or, alternatively, wild roses, sloe, hawthorn or holly.

You can also put standard (or espalier or cordon possibly) fruit trees in your garden.

It's better to choose old-fashioned varieties which are now available in certain nurseries. The following are particularly robust and do not require too much attention: Laxton Superb, which is lovely and crisp, Egremont Russet, a heavy cropper, or Lord Lambourne, which is a perfect eating and stewing apple.

Allow some space for a few clusters of hardy flowering plants and space on the wall for climbing plants.

You can also choose plants which are more fussy about the type of soil or the amount of sunlight they need, but be careful to make sure that you give them what they need. Don't let them be overpowered by a plant which is either too near or too greedy.

For the enthusiast.

You have definitely been bitten by the gardening bug. Each day you go out and look at your plants. In the winter you organize the return of spring; in the summer you train plants which are in a mess. You follow the growth and progress of your plants closely and you'll do anything to help them along.

By ensuring that they don't come to any harm by pruning here and there to check their growth, you can bring an enormous number of different species into your garden.

Go on, try it out! All sorts of combinations are possible. Plants have an astonishing capacity to adapt to different conditions.

Keep a close eye on them and find out more. You'll find you'll improve your garden and your gardening skills.

Try the following fruit trees in the form of espaliers: apricots, apples, pears and cherries. Learn how to train and prune them – they'll look so pretty on your walls among the trees. Their crop of fruit will be a particular joy for you.

Make room for all types of plants in front of and between your trees...

If you're lucky enough to have a sunny garden, one or two tall trees can be planted alongside climbing plants, espaliers and shrubs, as long as each gets a little sun some time in the day. For this reason, it's best to plan carefully what you are going to plant. For instance, if currant bushes take up the edges of your flower beds you can mix them with tall flowers which like the shade.

Keep the walls least exposed to the sun and the corners for non-fruit varieties. Choose small delicate bushes which don't take up too much space. Control their growth, so you can put in other plants as well. Certain trees can be pruned into hedgerows which can be particularly delightful.

My tips.

When you tackle your winter pruning and tidying don't throw away the clippings. I separate the leaves from the thicker branches and put these into the compost heap.

Cut the end of overgrown branches using a pair of pruning shears to about 20in (50cm) and form them into bunches. The following spring they can be used as protection for the young shoots, as well as for stakes for plants which are slightly too spindly. Cats will certainly not be able to get through these natural barriers.

For hedgesparrows and chaffinches I have made a birdbox and have tied it at a height of 10-12ft (3-4m) on the trunk of a silver birch.

TABLE I

Trees noted for their blossom.

Trees 20-60ft (6-18m).

Species	CROWN	GROWTH	PRICKLY	EDIBLE	SCENTED	BEST TIME OF YEAR
False Acacia / Robinia pseudoacacia	upright crown	fast growth	prickly	edible	scented	V-VI
Cultivated Cherry	broad crown	fast growth		edible		IV-V
Wild Cherry / Prunus avium	upright crown	fast growth		edible		IV+VII
Flowering Ash / Fraxinus ornus	broad crown	fast growth			scented	IV-VI
Indian Bean Tree / Catalpa bignonioides	broad crown					VII-VIII
Whitebeam / Sorbus aria	upright crown				scented	V+IX

Trees 10-25ft (3-7m).

Species	CROWN	GROWTH	PRICKLY	EDIBLE	SCENTED	BEST TIME OF YEAR
Scotch Laburnum / Laburnum alpinum	broad crown				scented	V-VI
Mountain Ash / Sorbus aucuparia	broad crown					V+X
Paulownia / Paulownia tomentosa	broad crown	slow growth		edible	scented	IV-V
Cherry Plum / Prunus cerasifera	broad crown	slow growth				III-IV
Cultivated Apple	broad crown	slow growth		edible		III-IV
Judas Tree / Cercis siliquastrum	broad crown					V
Cultivated Plum	broad crown	slow growth		edible		III-IV
Bird Cherry / Prunus padus	broad crown				scented	V
Hawthorn / Crataegus monogyna	broad crown		prickly	edible	scented	V+X
Snowy Mespilus / Amélanchier lamarckii	broad crown	slow growth		edible		III-IV
Garden Pear / Pyrus communis	broad crown	slow growth		edible		IV-V
Flowering Crab Apple / Malus "Profusion"	broad crown			edible	scented	IV-V
Cornelian Cherry / Cornus mas	broad crown			edible		III+IX

Key

- hardy
- broad crown
- upright crown
- slow growth
- fast growth
- prickly
- edible
- scented
- I – XII   best time of year

TREES

Shrubs and Bushes 6-12ft (2-4m).

Name	GROWTH	PRICKLY	EDIBLE	SCENTED	BEST TIME OF YEAR
Butterfly Bush — Buddleia davidii	✓			✓	VII-IX
Mexican Orange Blossom — Choisya ternata	✓		✓		V
Tree Hollyhock — Hibiscus syriacus	✓				VII-X
Carpenteria — Carpenteria californica	✓				VI-VII
Broom — Cytisus scoparius	✓			✓	V-VI
Barberry — Berberis darwinii	✓	✓	✓		IV+X
Bladder Senna — Colutea arborescens	✓				IV-V
Witch Hazel — Hamamelis mollis					XII-II
Medlar — Mespilus germanica		✓	✓		V-VI
Quince — Cydonia oblonga	✓		✓		V
Mock Orange — Philadelphus coronarius	✓			✓	VI-VII
Vibernum — Vibernum burkwoodii	✓			✓	IV-V
Snowball Bush — Vibernum opulus	✓				IV+X
Mahonia — Mahonia japonica	✓			✓	XII
Camellia — Camellia japonica	✓			✓	III-V
St. John's Wort — Hypericum "Hidcote"	✓				VII-IX

Shrubs and Bushes 1½-5ft (0.5-1.5m).

Name	GROWTH	PRICKLY	EDIBLE	SCENTED	BEST TIME OF YEAR	
Fishbone Cotoneaster — Cotoneaster horizontalis	✓				V-VI	**Sun-loving**
Flowering Currant — Ribes sanguineum	✓			✓	III-IV	
Shrub Roses — Rosa centifolia, Rosa rugosa, Rosa rubiginosa	✓	✓	✓	✓	V-VII	
Bell Heather — Erica cinerea					VI-IX	
Heather — Calluna vulgaris					V-IX	
Bridal Wreath — Spiraea arguta	✓				IV-V	**Tolerate shade**
Deutzia — Deutzia rosea				✓	V-VI	
Shrubby Cinquefoil — Potentilla fruticosa					V-IX	
St. John's Wort — Hypericum inordorum "Elstead"				✓	VI-IX	**Shade-loving**
Skimmia — Skimmia japonica	✓				III-IV	

TABLE II

Trees noted for their foliage.

Trees 20-60ft (6-18m).

Name	CROWN	GROWTH	PRICKLY	EDIBLE	SCENTED	BEST TIME OF YEAR
Walnut — Juglans regia	broad crown	fast growth		edible		
Oak — Quercus robur	broad crown	slow growth				
Horse chestnut — Aesculus hippocastanum	broad crown	fast growth				V
Poplar — Populus tremula	upright crown	fast growth				IX-X
Sweet chestnut — Castanea sativa	broad crown	fast growth		edible		
Silver Birch — Betula pendula	upright crown	fast growth				IX-X
Lime — Tilia cordata	broad crown	fast growth		edible	scented	VI
Larch — Larix decidua	upright crown	fast growth			scented	IV+IX
Copper Beech — Fagus purpurea	broad crown	slow growth		edible		V-VI
Red Oak — Quercus rubra	broad crown	fast growth				IX-X
Alder — Alnus glutinosa	upright crown	fast growth				IV

Trees 10-25ft (3-7m).

Name	CROWN	GROWTH	PRICKLY	EDIBLE	SCENTED	BEST TIME OF YEAR
Mulberry — Morus nigra	broad crown	fast growth		edible		
Field Maple — Acer campestre	broad crown	fast growth				IX-X
Common Hornbeam — Carpinus betulus	broad crown	slow growth				IV-V
Kilmarnock Willow — Salix caprea	broad crown	fast growth			scented	IV-V
Maple — Acer negundo	broad crown	fast growth				IX-X

Key

	hardy
	broad crown
	upright crown
	slow growth
	fast growth
	prickly
	edible
	scented
I – XII	best time of year

Shrubs 6-12ft (2-4m).

Plant	GROWTH	PRICKLY	EDIBLE	SCENTED	BEST TIME OF YEAR
Sea Buckthorn — *Hippophae rhamnoides*		✓	✓		XI-XII
Japanese Pagoda Tree — *Sophora japonica*	✓				III
Hazel — *Corylus avellana*	✓		✓		II-III
Privet — *Ligustrum vulgare*	✓				IX-X
Oleaster — *Elaeagnus augustifolia*		✓		✓	
Japanese Maple — *Acer palmatum*	✓				IX-X
Snowberry — *Symphoricarpos*	✓				VII-VIII
Common Spindle — *Euonymus europaeus*	✓				VIII

Bushes 1½-5ft (0.5-1.5m).

Plant	GROWTH	PRICKLY	EDIBLE	SCENTED	BEST TIME OF YEAR	
Blackcurrant — *Ribes nigrum*	✓		✓	✓	VII	**Sun-loving**
Redcurrant — *Ribes rubrum*	✓		✓		VI	
– red variety					VI	
– white variety						
Gooseberry — *Ribes uva-crispa*	✓	✓	✓		VI	
Raspberry — *Rubus idaeus*	✓	✓	✓		VI	**Tolerate shade**
Blackberry — *Rubus fruiticosus*	✓	✓	✓	✓	IX	
Woolly Willow — *Salix lanata*	✓				IV	
Bilberry — *Vaccinium myrtillus*	✓		✓		IX-X	**Shade-loving**
Swamp Blueberry — *Vaccinium corymbosum*	✓		✓		IX	
Cranberry — *Vaccinium vitis idaea*	✓		✓		VIII-IX	

TABLE III

Evergreen trees.

Trees 50ft (15m) or more.	CROWN	GROWTH	PRICKLY	EDIBLE	SCENTED	BEST TIME OF YEAR
Monkey Puzzle *Araucaria araucana*	broad crown					
Scots Pine *Pinus sylvestris*	upright crown	slow growth			scented	IV-V
Incense Cedar *Libocedrus decurrens*	upright crown	slow growth			scented	
Austrian Pine *Pinus nigra*	upright crown	fast growth			scented	
Yew *Taxus baccata*	broad crown	slow growth			scented	IV-V

Trees 15-30ft (5-10m).	CROWN	GROWTH	PRICKLY	EDIBLE	SCENTED	BEST TIME OF YEAR
Juniper *Juniperus communis*	upright crown	slow growth		edible		IX-X
Gum Tree *Eucalyptus gunnii*	broad crown	fast growth			scented	VII-VIII
Common Holly *Ilex aquifolium*	upright crown	slow growth	prickly			IX-II
Korean Fir *Abies Koreana*	upright crown	fast growth			scented	V

Key

- hardy
- broad crown
- upright crown
- slow growth
- fast growth
- prickly
- edible
- scented
- I – XII   best time of year

Shrubs 6-12ft (2-4m).

Plant	GROWTH	PRICKLY	EDIBLE	SCENTED	BEST TIME OF YEAR
Mountain Pine — Pinus mugo	●			●	
Myrtle — Myrtus communis	●			●	V-VII
Escallonia — Escallonia "Apple Blossom"	●				VI-IX
Fatsia — Fatsia japonica	●				X
Common Box — Buxus sempervirens	●			●	

Bushes 1½-5ft (0.5-1.5m).

Plant	GROWTH	PRICKLY	EDIBLE	SCENTED	BEST TIME OF YEAR
Rock Rose — Cistus laurifolius					VI-VII
Bearberry — Arctostaphylos uva-ursi					IV-V
Daphne — Daphne odora				●	II-III
Veronica — Hebe brachysiphon					VI-VII
Common Gorse — Ulex europaeus	●	●		●	V-VII
Lavender — Lavandula spica	●			●	VII-IX
Alexandrian Laurel — Danae racemosa	●				X

Sun-loving

Tolerate shade

Shade-loving

WALLS OR HEDGES, BORDERS,
A SITTING-OUT AREA

WALLS.

Our little town gardens are often surrounded by high walls. This feature is sometimes criticized: it seems individualist; you feel enclosed; the garden looks tiny; it limits the things you can grow. A big communal garden would be much nicer.

Walls as a supply of heat.

I think the advantages of walls far outweigh these slight drawbacks.

First of all, they provide an extra supply of heat. In town, growth of plants is two weeks ahead of that in the country. Frost is less severe and the heat stored and given off by our walls allows the cultivation of types of plants more susceptible to frost, like apricot trees. In spring the growth of young plants is accelerated, giving them the necessary headstart to help them survive the increasing shade of the foliage. In summer, plants that need heat, like hollyhock, scabious or delphinium, will grow better against walls.

Walls are also very useful for espalier fruit trees, and to train climbers against, increasing the planting possibilities in a small area (see the chapter on "Trees").

Walls as nature reserves.

Finally, if the walls are covered with greenery, and as long as you don't try to make them waterproof by painting them, they also make an excellent nature reserve. Ivy, clematis, honeysuckle and blackberry will grow over them to provide welcome refuge for birds that like to nest in dark places or those that nest low. Numerous types of useful spiders and insects will settle in the cracks and crevices.

You will be completely convinced of the usefulness of walls after you have discovered a little coal-tit clinging to the wall like an acrobat, nimbly hopping about in search of food, or when you find beautiful spiders' webs full of trapped insects.

Walls cast their shadow on the garden at certain times of day. An additional benefit! This allows a much greater variety of plants in a very small area.

A few small drawbacks.

In summer, walls that get the sun give off a great deal of heat, so the plants need watering every evening.

The soil dries out much more quickly in these places. You must take care to maintain the humus level so that the soil retains the water better when it is very hot (see the chapter "Sunlight and the Layout of Your Garden").

Some plants take some time to get used to this alternating sun

and shade. For the first few years they have a tendency to become spindly and are more fragile. Feed them well with a good compost; they will then adapt much better.

When your walls are covered with greenery you will have some additional work training the espaliers and cleaning.

Maintain your garden walls or leave them alone?

The tidy-minded are dismayed when they look at their garden walls in winter. This is generally the time when they decide to repaint them the following spring.

I have advised all my friends to do nothing of the sort, and they are glad they listened to me.

This option has aesthetic as well as practical advantages:

faded and weathered paint makes the walls much less conspicuous. A little less neatness is better suited to the fauna and flora of our gardens. The mixture of lime and earth used in the past to cover walls is slightly friable and this is good for insects and birds.

Natural brick is a porous and living material, a few little cracks are altogether a good idea. As long as the bricks don't fall out, it is unnecessary to repoint them. Leave the brick natural! If it really upsets you, whitewash it, but don't use paint.

It is also important to keep the ridge tiles on the wall in good condition. They should be sloping to prevent water collecting in the wall. (Fig. 1)

Faithful old wisteria.

We've already mentioned espalier fruit trees, but on our walls we also find wisteria that is sometimes very old. This plant is extremely sturdy. I have seen some planted in a small hole in a terracotta tile climbing up several storeys of a house. In spring it is advisable, but not essential, to cut back the new wisteria shoots, removing three or four buds. This will encourage the next flowering. You can also contain your wisteria's growth a little, but avoid doing anything too drastic. The wisteria won't like it! Branches too severely pruned often die.

Evergreen ivy.

More rarely, you will still find ivy on the garden wall or the wall of the house. In the past it was given pride of place; nowadays, it is much maligned. But its bad reputation is a little undeserved. On solid walls and a fascia in good condition, it doesn't cause any damage. Its tangle of growth can keep a delapidated wall standing. There is an enormous advantage in growing ivy: it is a paradise for birds, particularly nightingales.

Contrary to popular belief, ivy is not a parasite feeding off the trees it grows on. The walls of our buildings, often dreary on the garden-facing side, would surely look more cheerful if ivy was introduced. It grows in the smallest

hole in the ground. If it becomes too thick, you can cut it back at the end of the winter before the birds start nesting, and clean the surrounds of your windows. You must not be frightened of spiders; they also deserve rehabilitation as they feed on numerous insects. Besides, in this country, none of them are poisonous or dangerous.

Maintain the base and the ridges of walls.

On the other hand, you should keep an eye on the bottom 12-15in (30-40cm) of the wall. Repoint if necessary. It is from here that any risk of the wall collapsing arises.

fig 1

Old roses.

Sometimes in our gardens we're lucky enough to find an old species of either a climbing rose or a shrub rose. "Mme Pierre Oger" is a rosy pink, very fragrant shrub rose that flowers freely throughout the summer. "Dorothy Perkins" is a vigorous rambler and produces clusters of rose-pink blooms early in summer. They produce a lot of flowers; their faded petals have an unmatched charm and they are much more delicately scented than our modern roses.

You certainly must not remove these roses, even if they are very old. An old rose can recover very easily. Cut back its weak branches a little and feed regularly with a good manure. Within two or three years, you will see it flourish and grow new shoots again. You can also try to take cuttings or layer it during August or September. This is quite easy to do. Some kinds of roses put out suckers at the base. You can detach these new shoots and then replant them elsewhere.

Your old rose is bare round the base? Never mind! Simply plant another shrub underneath it, such as philadelphus, a lower-growing rose-bush or a clematis: the effect is astonishing. You must just be careful that they don't smother each other.

COVER YOUR WALLS WITH CLIMBERS.

In nurseries that specialize in old roses, you can find numerous delightful species of shrub rose, old and modern, or climbing rose. [1]

Rose-bushes prefer a sunny position, a wall facing south, south-east or south-west; otherwise they are more susceptible to diseases such as mildew, and they flower poorly.

On well-exposed walls you could also grow a vine. These are fun to grow. Vines grow quickly but you must learn how to prune them. Hard pruning is essential if you want to get grapes.

On less sunny walls, even behind shrubs and trees, plant ivy or Virginia creeper (don't let it wind round trees, it smothers them), different types of bramble, with or without thorns, such as American blackberry; they grow anywhere and produce a lot of fruit.

Honeysuckle and small-flowered clematis.

In slightly shady places that do get

1. See the list at the end of this book for old-fashioned rose specialists.

a few rays of sunshine, honeysuckle does very well. It smells so fragrant in the morning and in the evening when it is in flower!

Clematis needs a north, north-east or north-west aspect to do well. It doesn't like heavy soil or too much soil. The roots need shade and sufficient moisture.

I prefer small-flowered clematis, closely related to the hedgerow clematis – wild, white and very fragrant. It has more blooms, denser foliage, and grows quicker and better. Clematis alpina, for instance, is periwinkle blue and the first to flower, in the month of March. Its flowering over, it produces pretty feathery tufts that last all the rest of the year. Clematis montana produces a cascade of little pale pink flowers in the month of May.

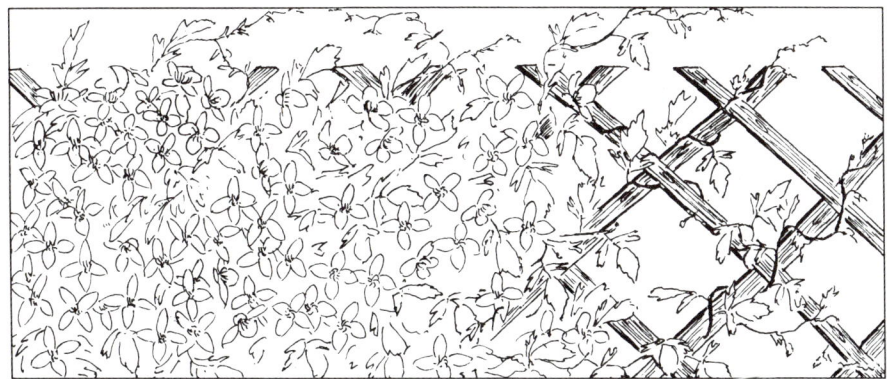

How to plant climbers.

Like trees, climbers can be planted throughout the dormant period. However, I prefer to plant rose-bushes at the end of winter. Follow the instructions given for planting trees, but the hole that you dig can be smaller.

You will also have to provide some support for your climbing plants. You can use wooden trellis frames for light plants; for others, extend lengths of wire and attach the plants to these as they grow. For clematis and honeysuckle, you can attach a piece of wide-mesh trellis, 2-3ft (0.7-1m) square, to the wall; it will quickly disappear beneath the greenery. Vines and Virginia creeper need no support; they can attach themselves.

A few suggestions for less common climbers.

Table IV on page 62 suggests various species of shrubs and climbers that are becoming less common or are less well known to the public.

To help you choose, they have been classified into four categories:

Plants with fragrant flowers.
Plants with non-fragrant flowers.
Plants more notable for their foliage.
Evergreens.

As for other types of plant, they are classified according to their need for light. In the columns you will find symbols indicating:

Whether the plant is edible.
Whether the plant has thorns.
Its speed of growth.
Its maximum height.
The flowering season.

HEDGES.

Lucky gardeners in residential areas, on the outskirts of our towns, have gardens with hedges. Hedges have numerous advantages: they make the garden look bigger; they make it greener and cooler; they attract numerous birds. These natural boundary-markers also encourage the presence of small frogs, hedgehogs and even squirrels. Gardens like this are especially suitable for establishing little ponds.

One is generally obliged to put up fences or to plant hedges to mark the boundaries between gardens. Sometimes, there is even a series of rules attached to this: the height of the fence or hedge, the distance for planting out that has to be observed, and so on.

Hedges need slightly more regular maintenance than walls. In our towns, hedges cannot be left to grow unchecked. They have to be trimmed a little.

Today the fashion is usually for hedges to be uniform, of privet or thuja. What is more, they are rigorously square-cut. A deplorable fashion! We have lost the

habit of introducing variety into our hedges. Look at country hedgerows: made up of different species, teeming with animal life and at the foot of them, a flourishing flora, rich in beauty and variety. Full of smells and rustling, these hedgerows are both charming and useful. But nowadays, all you see is beaten earth at the foot of uniform hedges that are trimmed in straight lines.

How to improve a hedge that is lacking in charm.

Privet hedges would be much prettier if left to grow a bit wild and to flower. There is nothing to stop you introducing other types of shrub here and there: hazel, blackthorn, Rosa rugosa, beech, symphoricarpos.

Perhaps you have a traditional thuja hedge that gives you some privacy in winter and summer. If you are lucky enough to have the "occidentalis" variety (less ornamental, it goes brown in winter), you will have some consolation since it attracts numerous birds to nest. If you are tired of your thuja hedge, you, too, can introduce some different well-chosen species here and there.

Long live the country hedge!

You can introduce an old-fashioned country hedge and enjoy its benefits, the variety of its foliage, the domestic use that can

be made of certain shrubs, the return of birds and butterflies – in short, the ecological equilibrium that it establishes by its presence. At the foot of your hedge, you will see various wild flowers reappearing. Leave them alone! They are an additional charm.

How to create a country hedge.

A very great variety of trees and

shrubs can be used for this purpose. They are all hardy plants. Many of them have thorns and I have always experienced a certain pleasure in wrestling with their thorns when it comes to cutting the hedge. It at least gives you the chance to have a good swear, both at your own clumsiness and your scratches.

Depending on your taste, you can select two or three different types – or more if the length of your hedge allows it – alternating them as you plant them. You can try mixing hornbeam, hawthorn, blackthorn and purple hazel. Another good mix is berberis, privet, cherry laurel, dog rose, syringa and espalier pear. Or else simply choose a basic hedge and then alternate every 5ft (1.5m)

with, for instance, a selection of hornbeam, dotted here and there with blackthorn, elder (excellent against aphids), holly and amelanchier.

How to plant your informal hedge.

The instructions given for trees apply to hedges. But take the

precaution of ordering the plants in advance, especially if you want some different and less common varieties. Young saplings of about 2ft (80cm) should ideally be planted 1½ft (50cm) apart, in staggered rows, in holes 1ft (30cm) wide by 1ft (30cm) deep. After planting, place a good mulch of manure or compost around the shrubs. This will help them to root well and will retain the moisture essential to young plants during the first year.

Trimming an informal hedge.

During the first year there will be no need to trim your young plants. You could possibly trim a little off the lateral branches in order to strengthen them and to encourage the shrub to throw out new shoots.

After two or three years, your hedge should be trimmed at least once a year, preferably in July or August. If you trim it twice, the second time should be at the beginning of April.

For this job I prefer to use secateurs or gardening shears: you can see what you are doing better than if you use an electric hedge-cutter, which anyway damages the new shoots by tearing them.

Finally, a country-style hedge should not be trimmed severely. Slightly undisciplined bushes are much more appropriate in a town garden.

The trimmings will go on to your compost heap. If your hedge is very long it would be worth getting a compost shredder. This machine cuts the trimmings into little pieces which decompose much more easily.

A few suggested species particularly suitable for hedges.

All the species suggested for hedges can also be planted individually as ornamental trees. What distinguishes them, above all, is their vigorous habit and their ability to tolerate trimming and close planting, which doesn't suit most trees.

They are categorized in Table V into four sections:

Thorny species to serve as a deterrent.
Species noted for their blossom.
Species more noted for their foliage.
Evergreens.

As in the preceding tables, a symbol indicates which ones are edible; rapidity of growth; and the flowering season.

ORGANIZATION OF BORDERS AND THE SITTING-OUT AREA.

Let's look now at how to organize your borders around the space that you leave free in the middle of your garden. You should plant borders of varying depths along the walls, so that your central area is defined by these different borders.

In a small garden...

A fairly deep border, 2-3ft (0.8-1m), will be planted along the sunniest wall. It could be much deeper, if this wall is at the bottom of the garden.

If you have a long garden, a narrower border than the first can be planted along the second less sunny wall. You may also decide to plant it with trees and bushes,

in groups or individually. A large space could be reserved at the bottom of the garden or near the top for varied planting or for a pond. It is not necessary to define this space too strictly.

The plan of your garden will then be more or less similar to:
Figure 2, if the sun shines mainly on the far wall.
Figure 3, if the left-hand wall gets more sun.

Figure 4, if it is the right-hand wall that enjoys the warmth of the sun.

If your garden is long and narrow.

You may also decide to weave a little path between a series of well-stocked borders and shrubs. Take care to arrange your plants so you leave enough space in the central area.

How to edge your borders.

It is not essential to edge all borders, although edging makes it easier to keep a garden tidy and helps with positioning certain low-growing plants. It will be necessary along a path made of gravel.

Edgings should be used depending on their necessity, so that the eye is attracted by the plants, rather than by the edge itself. Vary the materials used, according to the situation, so as to avoid monotony.

For instance, a rough stone edge will provide support for rock plants and set them off prettily. One made of tiles could be used to separate a path from a border planted with currant bushes and strawberry plants intermingled with herbs. A wooden edge could be used to surround rose-bushes or a shrubbery.

A narrow border against a wall, planted mainly with shrubs, will be

more attractive to look at if the edge is not too severe. Put an edge here that is sunken so it doesn't protrude too much. You could also simply bank up the soil once a year.

Simple materials for edging a border.

Both sophisticated and artificial materials are not really in keeping with nature and their effect will often be disappointing.
You can use:
Old sandstone tiles set at an angle. (Fig. 5)
Pieces of wood trimmed in an original fashion and soaked in preservative. (Fig. 5)
A fir-tree log laid on its side and kept in position with stakes. (Fig. 5)
Logs of wood measuring about 1ft (30cm), lined up next to each other. (Fig. 5)

To edge wide borders, rough

stones are unobtrusive and practical. I personally prefer sandstone because of its strange, rounded shapes and its pretty ochre shades. Also, it is fairly porous, which makes it more compatible with all kinds of tiny animal and vegetable life-forms. Flint stones are another very natural-looking alternative.

A border can also be defined simply by raising the height of the turfed area in the middle of the garden. In this case, the turfed area should be trimmed all around with a spade once a year to reshape the raised ground.

You can also construct a little raised rockery, in a well-exposed corner, where you can grow your herbs and rock-flowers. Ideally, you should build a low drystone wall (with the stones simply placed one on top of the other). It should then be filled in with heathland soil. As the plants grow, their roots will spread between the stones.

How to position your edging correctly.

If the border to be edged is straight, you should stretch a piece of string between two stakes and mark out the line with the cutting ege of a spade. If your edging has to follow a curve, this marking out can be done directly with the spade.

You should dig a trench slightly wider than the material to be used and about 4in (10cm) deep. Stones should be buried to two-thirds of their height; tiles, a half or more. Finally, place whatever material you are using in this trench, then fill in with earth, packing it well so that the edging stays in place. (Fig. 8)

fig 8

A CLEARING AMONG YOUR PLANTS.

The size of this will depend on the space you have allocated to borders and the actual size of your garden. Don't place it right in the middle. It's more natural-looking on one side or the other of the garden – and be sure to give it an asymmetrical shape.

Too much geometrical neatness does nothing for a small, enclosed garden!

If the sitting-out area is quite big, or long and thin, it could be enhanced by some small trees or a shrubbery. You could create a shady area or a pond in a sunny corner. A stone bench, or one made of wood or wrought iron, could be placed in the shady spot.

Meadow or lawn?

Lawn! It is a real fad these days – everyone wants their own patch of lawn.

Alas, this presents certain difficulties in town gardens. The amount of shade and acidity of the soil are two major problems. It will often take several years and a lot of trouble to get a more or less acceptable lawn. Then it will have to be regularly treated against being overrun with moss and fed with fertilizer. It will also have to be watered during the summer, scarified [2] and spiked with a fork to aerate it from time to time. And it will also need cutting several times during the summer.

The lawn will tend to grow sparsely underneath trees and where you regularly walk. If the access to your sitting-out area is narrow, lay stepping stones, using either flat stones or old tiles.

To cut your lawn opt for a good-quality handmower because it cuts without tearing out the grass. It is light and not very noisy and for such a small area it really is not tiring.

2. *Scarify: to rake the lawn vigorously to remove dead grass and compacted matter.*

Don't be too obsessed about keeping the lawn in immaculate condition. A few weeds, daisies and dandelions make the lawn more lively and mean that you can let it grow longer between cuts. You will end up with more of a little flower-filled meadow, that will be more robust than an English-style lawn. And you'll be much more popular with the local birds, bees and insects.

Gravel.

There is another way to cover the central area of small gardens. That is to lay down gravel. This is hardly ever done, yet this solution has several advantages. It is ideal for shady gardens because:

This type of surface reflects light and heat better.

It needs no maintenance apart from an occasional rough raking.

It allows insects and earthworms to circulate freely.

For this kind of surface, I prefer fairly small pebbles. I like the mixtures of browns and blacks. They are also smooth, less unpleasant underfoot than large stones and more fun to look at with all their different sizes and shapes.

You can also use roughly-pounded brick, but this is messy.

To combat the growth of weeds among the pebbles, you can spray them with some boiling hot water or nettle juice [3].

3. *Nettle juice: see the recipe in the "My Tips" section of the chapter on "Pruning and Garden Maintenance".*

Flagstones or paving stones.

If it is small, the sitting-out area can also be covered with paving stones, either irregular or rectangular, of different sizes. In this case, it is best to leave space between them to allow a little grass, moss, or pearlwort to grow – they love shade and dampness.

These three types of ground cover can be used to make a winding path through the garden.

My suggestions for the idle gardener.

Don't paint your scruffy walls! Leave them natural and faded. Choose climbers to cover them that don't need trimming: ivy, Virginia creeper, honeysuckle, thornless bramble.

Continue to use the contrasting varieties of plants to obtain changing effects. If you are not afraid of thorns, an old rose-bush in a corner with good light will add a touch of beauty. Plant a peony bush, they are all superb and so fragrant! Put a clematis montana or clematis alpina in a west-facing position; they grow all by themselves.

If you have to replace a fence or wall – or if you feel energetic enough – then planting a hedge is one of the easiest ways of encouraging wildlife. Choose thornless bushes that don't grow too big: hornbeam, beech, viburnum, hazel, euonymus europaeus or symphoricarpos.

For your borders, use fir-tree logs or sandstone rocks.

Make life easier for yourself by doing without a lawn. Put down gravel or paving stones. Don't forget to make room for a seat in the most pleasant spot and – why not? – a fixed table at which you will be able to sit outside to eat and to work.

For the occasional gardener.

If your garden is sunny, you could choose to plant old roses, a wisteria, a vine that for your purposes will, no doubt, be more aesthetic than practical, or an espaliered apricot just for the pleasure of watching it bloom.

Prepare your walls for climbing plants and espaliers by fixing wires or attaching mesh. Once this is done, you will have nothing more to do but tie up the odd branch from time to time.

If you feel inspired to start on a lasting, but practical, task you will enjoy edging your borders with more imagination. Build a rock garden or a pond with some aquatic plants such as water iris or myriophyllum.

You can also opt for a carpet full of "weeds", dandelions, daisies, crocuses. It will need cutting only in June and September. You can actually buy seed for a flowered lawn.

For the enthusiast.

You can grow anything against your wall: various espaliered fruit trees and all kinds of climbers: vine or climbing hydrangea ... intertwine the different plants. Train the shoots and espalier the branches. Your wall will soon disappear under greenery.

Plan to have lots of borders. You will never have enough space to put all your ideas into effect. You can erect a summer-house, train climbing plants to form an archway over paths or arrange a bower in a sunny corner. Here you can grow a Siberian pea tree, jasmine or miniature roses and annual climbing flowers.

If you decide to put a hedge around your garden, plant a protective old-fashioned country hedge with numerous thorny plants as well as fragrant species. Bees will come buzzing round happily and birds will settle in your garden.

My tips.

To support my plants I fix three lengths of strong wire along three walls of the garden, at a distance of 1½ft, 3ft and 5ft (50cm, 1m and 1.5m) respectively above the ground. To fix the wires, you need to cement hook eyes into the wall. Then the wire can be stretched with the aid of straining bolts placed just on one end.

To plant more climbers around the house, I took up several paving stones in the terrace. I dug out the soil to a depth of 18in (40cm) and climbing roses and clematis took root here.

A wooden archway enabled me to plant a vine at the far end of the terrace. It climbs up the wall of the house and forms a very pretty pergola in summer.

I made some nesting boxes for birds in an east-facing wall. At the top of the wall, below the ridge and safe from attack by cats, I took out a brick and replaced it with a wooden box of the same height and width, with a round hole 1½in (3.5cm) in diameter. It is removable, which means the nest can be cleaned in winter.

TABLE IV

Climbing plants or shrubs.

With fragrant flowers.

Plant	CROWN	GROWTH	PRICKLY	EDIBLE	SCENTED	BEST TIME OF YEAR
Wisteria — Wisteria sinensis	climbing crown	slow growth			scented	V-VI
Shrub roses — modern / old	shrub crown	fast growth	prickly	edible	scented	VI-VII
Climbing roses	climbing crown	slow growth	prickly		scented	VI-VII
Tree Peony — Paeonia suffruticosa	shrub crown				scented	V
Orange Peel Clematis — Clematis orientalis	climbing crown	fast growth				VII-X
Honeysuckle — Lonicera americana	climbing crown	fast growth			scented	VI-VII
Common Honeysuckle — Lonicera periclymenum	climbing crown	slow growth			scented	VI-VII

With non-fragrant flowers.

Plant	CROWN	GROWTH	PRICKLY	EDIBLE	SCENTED	BEST TIME OF YEAR
Winter Jasmine — Jasminum nudiflorum	shrub crown	slow growth			scented	XII-IV
Pea Tree — Caragana arborescens	shrub crown	slow growth				V
Alpine Clematis — Clematis alpina	climbing crown	fast growth				II-IV
Mountain Clematis — Clematis montana	climbing crown	fast growth				IV-V
Climbing Hydrangea — Hydrangea petiolaris	climbing crown					VI-VII
Bittersweet — Celastrus orbiculatus	climbing crown	fast growth				IX-X
Schizophragma — Schizophragma hydrangeoides	shrub crown	fast growth				VII

Key

- hardy
- climbing crown
- shrub crown
- slow growth
- fast growth
- prickly
- scented
- edible
- I – XII: best time of year

Noted for their foliage.

Evergreen.

Sun-loving

Tolerate shade

Shade-loving

	CROWN	GROWTH	PRICKLY	EDIBLE	SCENTED	BEST TIME OF YEAR
Grape vine — white — black	[icon]	[icon]		[edible]		
Kiwi Fruit — Actinidia chinensis *	[icon]	[icon]		[edible]		
Ornamental Vine — Vitis vinifera	[icon]	[icon]				IX-X
Virginia Creeper — Parthenocissus henryana	[icon]	[icon]				III-XI
Bramble — Rubus biflorus — Rubus cockburnianus — Rubus thibetanus	[icon]	[icon]		[edible]		IX-X

	CROWN	GROWTH	PRICKLY	EDIBLE	SCENTED	BEST TIME OF YEAR
Chilean Potato Tree — Solanum crispum	[icon]	[icon]				VI-X
Cotoneaster — Cotoneaster salicifolius	[icon]				[icon]	VI+X
Clematis — Clematis armandii	[icon]					III-IV
Common Ivy — Hedera helix	[icon]	[icon]				
Firethorn — Pyracantha atalantioides	[icon]		[prickly]			IX-X

* Needs a male and female plant to bear fruit.

HEDGES

TABLE V

Species suitable for informal hedges.

Key

	hardy
(symbol)	fast growth
(symbol)	slow growth
(symbol)	prickly
(symbol)	edible
(symbol)	scented
I – XII	best time of year

To act as a deterrent.

Species	GROWTH	PRICKLY	EDIBLE	SCENTED	BEST TIME OF YEAR
Dog Rose — Rosa canina	fast growth	prickly	edible	scented	V-VII
Rosa "Queen Elizabeth"	slow growth	prickly		scented	VI-VIII
Blackthorn/Sloe — Prunus spinosa	fast growth	prickly	edible		III-IV
Cherry Plum — Prunus cerasifera	fast growth	prickly	edible		IV
Hawthorn — Crataegus monogyna	fast growth	prickly	edible	scented	V
Barberry — Berberis darwinii	fast growth	prickly	edible		IV+X
Holly — Ilex aquifolium	fast growth	prickly	edible		IX-XII

Noted for their blossom.

Species	GROWTH	PRICKLY	EDIBLE	SCENTED	BEST TIME OF YEAR
Rosa rugosa	fast growth			scented	VI
Cherry Laurel — Prunus laurocerasus	slow growth			scented	IV
Medlar — Mespilus germanica	fast growth	prickly	edible		V-VI
Vibernum — Viburnum burkwoodii	fast growth			scented	IV-V
Briar Rose — Rosa rubiginosa	fast growth	prickly	edible	scented	V-VII

Noted for their foliage.

Evergreen.

	GROWTH	PRICKLY	EDIBLE	SCENTED	BEST TIME OF YEAR
Hornbeam Carpinus betulus	✿				
Common Elder Sambucus nigra	✿	🍴	✿		V+VIII
Hazel Corylus avellana "Aurea" Corylus maxima "Purpurea"	✿	🍴			III-IV
Oleaster Elaeagnus ebbingei	✿		✿		
Beech Fagus sylvatica	✿	🍴			

	GROWTH	PRICKLY	EDIBLE	SCENTED	BEST TIME OF YEAR
Common Ivy Hedera helix	✿				IX-X
Holly Ilex aquifolium	✿	🦎			IX-X
Box Buxus sempervirens	✿			✿	
Barberry Berberis darwinii	✿	🦎			IV+X
Arbor-vitae Thuja occidentalis	✿			✿	

All these species can also be used on their own as ornamental trees.

See tables I, II, III for characteristics.

FLOWERS AND HERBS

FLOWERS – THE FINERY OF OUR GARDEN.

Flowers add the final touch to our garden's array. It is they that give the garden its changing brilliance and the subtlest pinks and blues. Just when the garden looks dull an unexpected spray of yellow or red will decorate the border. And they continue to bloom one after another from the start of spring right through to the beginning of winter. It is the flowers too that surprise us with the variety of their shapes and their subtle fragrance.

Flowers – useful as well as beautiful.

There are wild flowers that have become familiar garden flowers, and other flowers from distant places that have become familiar medicines or herbs. There is an infinite variety of flowers, they all have their usefulness – from beauty to health to food.

There are many types of flower suitable for every inch of ground, dry or moist, sunny or shady. But they also have the ability to adapt remarkably well to where we plant them. Most of them will need a certain length of time to settle down. Often they struggle when they are first planted then, one fine day, perhaps a year later, sometimes even longer, you will see them flourish. Others, scorning the place you intended for them, will shamelessly go and settle a little further off.

The astonishing ability of plants to adapt.

Peonies are sun-loving plants. I dreamed of growing a Chinese smelling pink peony in my small garden. I bought myself a cluster and assigned it to a not very congenial position against a north-facing wall at the foot of a vigorous, young cherry tree. For the first two years it produced a few thin stalks with no strength in them and it did not flower. I stubbornly persisted in leaving it there, contenting myself with feeding it each year with my compost. Gradually, the cluster grew stronger. It has flowered for the past two years, a little later than my friend's peony, but with one advantage over her plant: its blooms, though less numerous, last much longer and it flowers over a longer period.

For three years, I tried to grow delphiniums at the end of my sunniest flower-bed, but in a very shady and dry spot beneath an already large silver birch, where supposedly nothing would grow, and, what's more, in the middle of currant bushes. The first year, I tried at the end of spring – too late! Slugs ate the young shoots; only a single sorry specimen survived. In late summer I put in a few new plants. Two-thirds of them survived the winter and flowered but their fragile stems bent and broke under the weight of their still-scraggy blooms. At the end of the following year, I put in another five or six plants in the same place. Now there are eleven and they all flower abundantly. The tallest are over 6ft (2m) and put out subsidiary spikes that flower after the main stem. The flowers are more graceful and less dense than if they were exposed to full sunlight all day.

A wealth of different flowers.

With flowers, even more than with trees and shrubs, you can take advantage of the wide range available. Flowers are used for decorating our homes and in all the main ceremonies of our culture. There is renewed interest in the hundreds of neglected, but delightful, wild flowers, such as red campion, herb Robert or comfrey. There are the less well-known

medicinal plants or herbs such as woodruff, angelica or sweet cicely. Flowers give us honey, too. But apart from their domestic usefulness, they are highly beneficial to our environment. Butterflies, bees, birds and insects all depend on flowers. So while you plant them for pure enjoyment, you will be benefitting a whole range of wildlife.

Learn to mix perennials in your garden with herbs and medicinal plants. Let a few "weeds" grow too – scarlet pimpernel, wood sorrel or creeping cinquefoil are all as delightful as our cultivated flowers.

Create winning combinations. The blooms of tea roses will be much more attractive if grown next to anemones De Caen, a red campion in flower, a cluster of valerian or a large cluster of sweet cicely. A pale columbine will

look magnificent next to purple irises and blackcurrant. Sweet william will go very well with fern, horseradish or a border of harebells. Globe flowers will make a charming contrast with a cluster of purple aconite alongside a cotoneaster covered with tiny pink flowers. Campanulas with their long supple stalks will go with branches of tarragon, marsh mallow or comfrey. Verbascum will complement rhubarb, and scarlet pimpernel will mingle discreetly with the rock rose in your borders. At the height of summer, the pastel shades of gladioli in abundance will stand out from the green of your flower-beds, while cosmos, of every shade of pink and red, will offset the great profusion of blooms on a few dahlias.

You will be the artist, the creator – every year you will modify and

Herbs and medicinal plants: woodruff, angelica, marjoram, hyssop.

improve your garden and the rate at which the flowers appear. It will be this slight degree of wildness in your scheme that will give your garden its originality. Personalized in this way, it will truly become your masterpiece.

Your flowers and the rhythm of the seasons.

During the winter season your flower-beds will be virtually empty. They will look very big, with only a few patches of green from one or two evergreens to break them up. You will have the impression that you could put in numerous different types of plant. Don't let yourself be taken in.

From now until the beginning of spring your very bare garden will be taking total advantage of

the sun and water available. It will be the first spring flowers that will benefit. Snowdrops, crocuses and daffodils will rapidly multiply. Primroses and tulips will be quick to appear before other plants put out their shoots. And within days, the irises will have to get used to the shade of spring trees already in leaf.

Before spring: planting and caring for your flowers.

During the quiet period before spring arrives, your perennials will be growing fast – you will see them increase in size day by day. For perennials to take full advantage of this period, it is important to plant them out before the end of winter – preferably in August or September when you've just bought them. Having been in the artificial environment of a nursery, the plants will be quite tender and they will need time to acclimatize

to the conditions in your garden.

Clumps of herbaceous perennials can be lifted and divided at the beginning of spring.

If you can get some young shoots from your friends' perennials, these can be transplanted in the spring and throughout the whole of summer. Try to keep some of the original soil around the roots and to plant the cuttings when it is overcast as they will take better; stormy weather is ideal. Then don't forget to water them until you see that they actually have taken.

Your perennial seedlings will benefit most from transplanting early in the summer. This will give them time to grow and establish themselves before winter. I replant carnations from spring to late summer, honesty in the month of May and hollyhocks in June. Obviously they must be kept in a place where they are not liable to be completely choked by other plants.

Similarly, you can plant hardy annual flowers all through spring until the beginning of summer.

Summer, the time to plan next year's flowers.

The beginning of summer is the best time to think about improving your garden and to decide what you are going to plant before winter closes in – and also in the following spring. Flower-beds are now overflowing with plants, but you will have been able to judge since the beginning of spring what is still missing: empty spaces where you could still slip in something; places where there is a lack of variety at certain times.

Now is the time to pick out the plants you wish to move at the end of summer, either because, despite all your efforts, they are doing badly, or their size means they'd look better elsewhere. Where low-growing or small plants are concerned, you can transplant them immediately with a clump of soil. In other cases, put a little plastic flag into the ground with the name of the plant written on it so as not to run the risk of not being able to find it again when the flowers have faded. As an extra precaution, also mark the place where you want to move it. (Fig. 1, opposite)

Before the winter, introduce new plants to your garden.

Now is the time to buy and put in most of the plants you have chosen during the summer, and any bulbs you want to flower in the spring.

Leave room among the flowers for herbs. Apart from their culinary usefulness, they are fragrant and pretty. You will be surprised by how majestic angelica can look, with its huge umbel, its fleshy stalks that can be preserved and served as an appetizer or used in

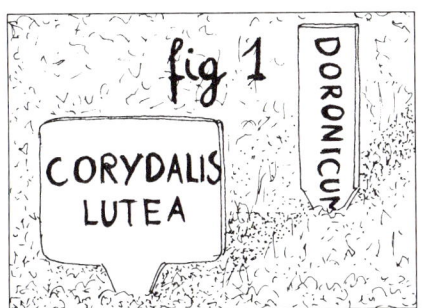

confectionery. It reseeds itself and does well anywhere. Fennel has a delicate foliage resembling asparagus, and looks lovely among other flowers in a sunny border. Clusters of burnet make an unusual border and it tastes good in salads. Mint will carpet the most barren corners of your garden. Woodruff will cover the ground in cool places and can be used to make an excellent aperitif. Rhubarb will screen your compost heap, which will help it to flourish. Wild strawberries will cover the ground of sunny borders that are shaded by shrubs.

Marjoram, hyssop and lavender will add discreet shades to your rockery borders. Comfrey and wild celery will give your garden a country look. They will be very useful for seasoning your soups. Chicory in blossom is an azure delight; garlic, onion and even leek have very decorative flowers.

Learn to recognize weeds.

You will see the strange barren strawberry, having strayed into your garden, vying with your wood strawberries, producing berries that are round, red and swollen, but insipid and incapable of developing into tasty berries.

These "weeds" are not liable to become too invasive. In our town gardens there is already so little space for all the plants we would like to grow, there is not much space left for unwanted plants. After you have got rid of thistles – by uprooting them, not by spraying – that thrive mainly on wasteland, you will see one or two "weeds" among your plants that you can't identify. By leaving them to grow, you will make lots of interesting discoveries.

I have adopted the habit of leaving one or two specimens of any shoots I don't recognize to grow. That is how this year I ended up with more than twenty-five different kinds of wild flower growing in my flower-tubs and borders. I had to buy a guide to wild flowers

to help me in my research. Apart from three little linden trees that came from goodness knows where, I am carefully nurturing two wild pear trees in an old winecase, plus a few other strangers until I find a good home for them.

It is as though these plants are gifted with powers of association. Chickweed always grows among newly-sown lettuce, parsley or sorrel. Red campion has estab-

"Weeds"? ... red campion (Silene dioica), scarlet pimpernel (Anagallis arvensis), wood sorrel (Oxalis acetosella), herb Robert (Geranium robertianum), barren strawberry (Potentilla sterilis).

lished itself in my garden next to two rose-bushes. Bindweed comes with petunias, wood sorrel seems to like geraniums, barren strawberries keep company with wood strawberries, mugwort and Queen Anne's thimble compete for space with tomato plants, corydalis grows alongside alyssum. I think they show good taste and I've left them to grow where they want. They complement my flowerpots and tubs.

And finally you can leave a

small patch of nettles totally untouched somewhere in a sunny patch. They're vital to the life-cycle of the butterfly.

Annual flowers are not as difficult as you might think!

Annual flowers are very useful for putting the finishing touches to your garden. Many of them are hardy, easy to sow and plant. Some seed themselves in the

most unexpected places. Generally, they do better here than in the places we choose for them. This is why I don't need to grow forget-me-not any more. It keeps reappearing in different places every year.

Cosmos and marigolds also tend to grow everywhere. From

time to time, a nasturtium that has escaped from the flower-tubs appears at the height of summer in the middle of a border, making a tremendous amount of greenery that winds endlessly among the plants. If you look hard, you will find a few little well-hidden nasturtium flowers! Petunias, once established, in following years will seed themselves haphazardly in other flower-tubs. When they are sufficiently well

grown – with three or four leaves – I replant them where I want them. Their bright blues and purples come as a wonderful surprise.

A few flowers that are easy to grow from seed.

Every year I add to my basic choice of flowers a few different annuals – nigella, verbena, morning glory, marigold, zinnia and sweet peas.

I buy some selected seeds at a good seed store to be sure of getting them to germinate. As early as the beginning of March, I sow my annual flowers in a hotbed on my terrace [1].

Growing from seed presents one small drawback: you can never be completely certain of success. By the time you realize the seeds haven't come up, it is sometimes too late to try again the same season, so you then have to do without the particular flower you have chosen. Alternatively, you can buy young plants of the desired species at a nursery.

Seeds gathered from mature flowers can be dried and kept in an old envelope placed in an airtight container. I have noticed that their ability to germinate is often better than that of bought seeds; they have shown no signs of the deterioration for which they are so often criticized.

The nice thing about growing from seed is that you end up with a whole series of young plants that you can give to your friends.

In order to grow from seed successfully, sow your seeds in a rich light soil. Keep it sufficiently moist.

Buying and planting annuals.

You can also obtain most annual flowers as young plants from

supermarkets and nurseries. They are not very expensive and are very practical for those who have little time to devote to gardening. They are often forced and so are more developed than those planted at home, but they grow more slowly when they are transplanted.

How to plant out seedlings.

The smallest seedlings will need to be transplanted twice.

1. As soon as they have three or four leaves, the small plants will need to be pricked off for the first time. For this, you can use the seedbox itself or another deeper tray will do.

These seedlings will take more vigorously if they are first dipped in a solution of water with a pinch of hormones for a few minutes.

2. The final planting out will take place when the young shoots have reached a height of about 4 in (10cm).

When planting out, you can sur-

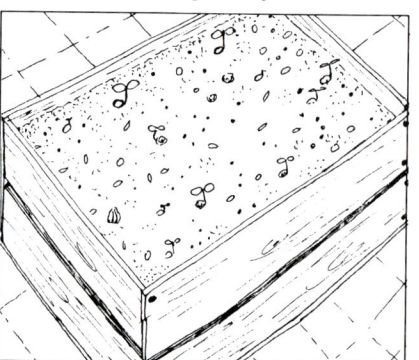

---

1. Hotbed: for details, see p.114 of chapter on "Pruning and Garden Maintenance".

round the young plant with a little fertilizer to encourage growth.

Every year I use the same seed-box measuring 2 ft 6 in x 2 ft 6 in (80cm x 80cm) to sow my flowers. It often happens that some seeds from the year before germinate by chance. I leave them to grow wherever they are without pricking them out. They develop more quickly and are stronger than my carefully nurtured seedlings. It is perfectly possible to transplant these vigorous young plants wherever you want them. They will take again just as well.

Planting out bare-root young plants.

The simplest way to do this is to use a dibber:

1. Press the dibber into loose soil, or soil loosened beforehand with a spade, so as to form a conical hole that will take the whole length of the roots. (Fig. 2)

2. While holding the plant vertically in the hole with one hand so that its neck is level with the surface, make a second hole with the dibber at an acute angle to the first. By returning the dibber to an upright position, the earth will be pushed against the roots of the plant. (Fig. 3) In this way the roots of the young plant are firmly packed into the soil without being subjected to too much handling, while a hole has been formed alongside it that allows water to

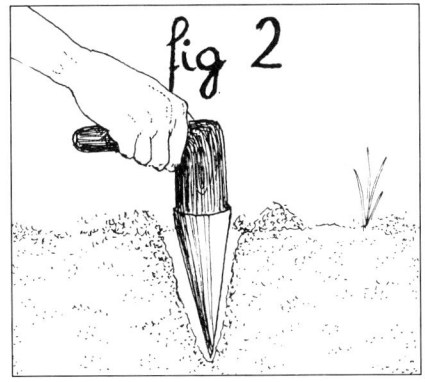

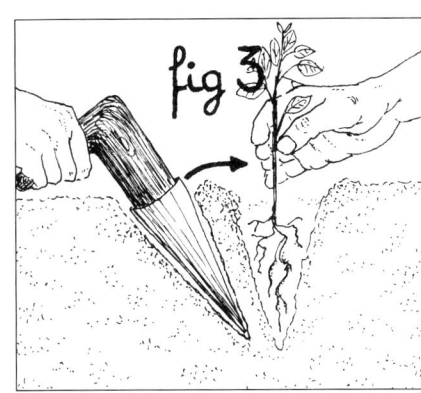

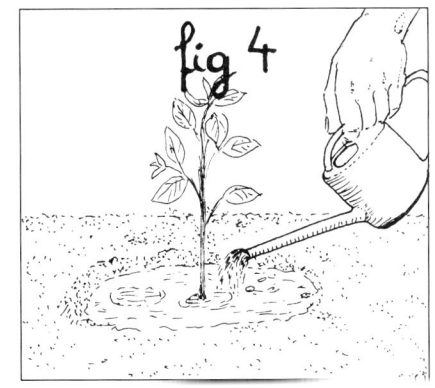

penetrate to the roots better. Left to itself, the hole will close up after a few waterings.

With a little practice, you will become very skilled at this job. Planting out can then be done very quickly.

Water your plants straightaway using a little watering-can with a long spout, taking care to water around the base of the fragile young plant. (Fig. 4)

How to plant young plants.

For this use a trowel. (Fig. 5) Dig a hole in earth that has been loosened beforehand. Your hole needs to be a little bigger than the pot or root ball of earth.

Before inserting the plant, make a few vertical incisions in the root ball with the cutting edge of the trowel to encourage the roots to spread. (Fig. 6) Then place the plant in the hole.

Don't put the plant in deeper than it was previously planted.

Set the root ball in the ground, holding it from below so as to be sure the roots are well positioned. (Fig. 7) Then gently fill in with soil, firm and, finally, water generously.

Plant in the evening, or better still in cloudy weather or in a light drizzle. During the first few weeks you should water the roots of the plants generously to prevent them drying out.

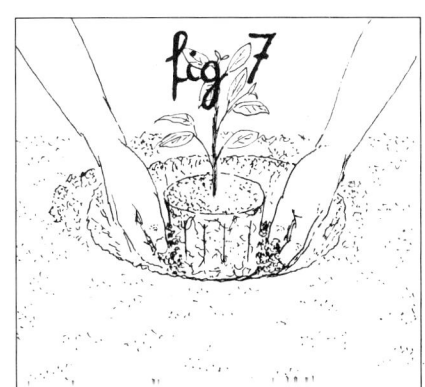

Border plants and dry-soil plants should be planted in a dry sunny position, as close as possible to stones to avoid rotting of the roots. Nevertheless, they will need to be well-watered when they are planted.

Your flowers like to be looked after.

Water them! If you have planted a lot of perennials in your garden, they will need regular watering in hot weather.

Water regularly and slowly to allow the water to penetrate, rather than giving an occasional flood.

Feed your weaklings! During the summer you can feed a little organic fertilizer to the plants that seem to be looking weak and straggly. For the others, an annual supply of compost will be enough.

Remove dead flower heads. Producing flowers tires the plant. Many types will grow more flowers once their dead flower heads have been removed. The plants will strengthen from the base and form new shoots for the following year.

Your flowering plant dies in the summer ...?

It suddenly wilts. There can be several reasons for this:

It was planted too late
Predators have fed on its leaves or roots
The position does not suit it.

Try to replant it in the same position at the end of summer before deciding to move it or to give up with this type of plant. It is not unusual after a first, failed attempt for the second to be crowned with success. You will also see some plants move themselves to a place that suits them; wild strawberry sends out its runners to where it will get more sun.

The production of flowers and fruit also depends on a series of other different factors and varies from year to year. Very often a whole region will have a bad apple season or everyone's roses do well. Some know-alls have the answers but seasonal disasters and successes remain unpredictable and will hold surprises in store for you.

Your hardy perennial disappears during the winter...?

Exposure to severe or extended frost, or too much rain can also lead to the destruction of perennials. Replant any survivors in a more sheltered or drier position.

Damage caused by voracious insects!

If your plants are suddenly devoured by in invasion of aphids or caterpillars, don't rush for the first pesticide to hand to deal with the problem. You will also destroy all the useful ladybirds and spiders. Moreover, the results will often be fairly unsatisfactory. If destroying the predators seems absolutely necessary, there are gentle methods that are just as effective and less destructive [2].

Slugs are an exception to this rule. Hedgehogs are the slugs'

2. *Gentle methods: see chapter on "Pruning and Garden Maintenance".*

enemy and if you lack this ally, you have a real problem. There are hundreds of failed suggestions, but transparent plastic bottles, with their bottoms cut off, do protect small plants. The best advice is to plant out when your seedlings have developed tough leaves. Slugs just don't enjoy tough, old leaves quite as much as juicy, tender ones.

If your garden has a rich variety of plants, insect attacks will remain very localized. And never mind about your only lupin being picked off each day this year by a mysterious predator before its flowers even open. Next year it will recover.

Don't forget to harvest useful plants.

Harvest your herbs and edible plants at the end of the summer, after they have flowered. Wash them in plenty of water and leave them to drain for a few hours out of reach of cats. Then you can dry them on a clean cloth for two or three weeks. Label each bundle of plants straightaway – when they have dried, you will no longer be able to distinguish them so easily. Then wrap them in cellophane and place them in airtight containers. You will be able to use them all winter until the following season.

You can also make syrup with

your fresh mint. All kinds of old recipes have come back into fashion: rosehip tea, elderberry and blackcurrant wine, etc.

Fill your house with flowers!

Annuals are the best to fill your vases with. They bear a lot of flowers and bloom at a time when the garden has been in flower for a while. But I don't like to deprive myself of the first splashes of beauty in the garden for the sake of my vases.

Cut your flowers early in the morning and put them into fresh water straightaway. You will notice that they last much longer.

If you like to enjoy the fragrance of your plants, don't go smelling them at midday, or you will be complaining that, in town, flowers have no fragrance. It is in the evening and the morning that they are at their most fragrant. In summer, go around your garden after a rainstorm and you will see.

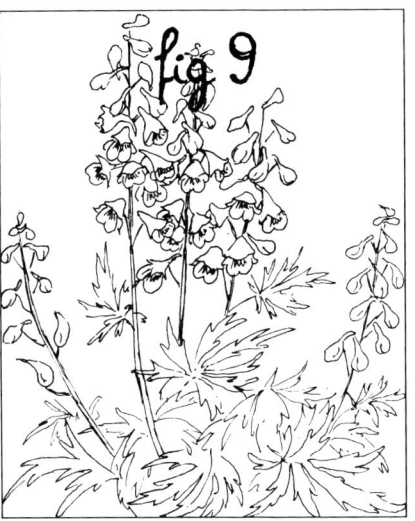

A selection of flowers to restore to glory.

To make it easy for you to choose, a selection of perennials have been classified according to appearance in three tables, starting on page 78. As with trees, they are categorized according to their maximum height and their need for shade or sunshine. In each table a symbol will tell you if the plant is edible, fragrant and the month of flowering. I have deliberately included in these tables herbs and medicinal plants together with ornamental flowers. A mixture in the garden is so much more attractive.

Table VI contains a selection of perennials with umbels or single flowers. (Fig. 8)
Table VII contains perennials with

flower clusters. (Fig. 9)
Table VIII groups together a few types of perennial rock plants. They only like a lot of sun, and a dry, light, coarse soil. If you try to plant them in rich, damp soil they will die off during the winter.
Table IX groups together a selection of bulbs and tubers. Some of these flower very early in the spring when nothing else is yet growing. This first touch of green is as necessary to us as to the insects which give them a warm welcome.

The other few plants grown from bulbs or tubers are summer plants that are precious at a time when the flowering of perennials is coming to an end.

All are vigorous and grow without any problem. With some of them the bulbs or tubers will need to be brought indoors during the winter; these are indicated by a symbol. The bulbs can be kept in the cellar or garage in a box filled with peat.
Table X gives annual flowers chosen for their readiness to grow easily and to thrive. In the table these flowers are followed by the symbol "seed" or "plant". When it seemed to me easier, or as easy, to sow them, the "seed" symbol follows immediately after the name, but when buying the plant is simpler than sowing, the name of the plant is followed by the "plant" symbol.

Here is an example of a public park, created by my "garden-architect", Anne van Horenbeeck. She has achieved a structured design that still gives free reign to nature – and encourages wildlife.

My suggestions for the idle gardener.

Sowing from seed, pricking out – in a word, growing annual plants – does not greatly appeal to you. Become a frequent visitor to those friends of yours who are gardening enthusiasts – you will be able to admire all these rather demanding, but very pretty, flowers in their gardens.

Opt for a few shrub roses. Limit yourself to robust perennial problem-free flowers, like meadow sweet, sedum, astilbe or campanula. For your borders, aubretia and alyssum, once established, will cause you no problems. Ground cover such as woodruff, St John's wort or periwinkle will suit you.

If you are a gourmet idler, take the trouble to build a little rockery where you can grow a few easy herbs such as wild thyme, winter savory, marjoram or tarragon.

Take particular care, when planting, to put your plants in a place that suits them best.

Don't be afraid of letting a few weeds grow among your shrubs and plants.

For the occasional gardener.

You too can make generous use of the more robust herbs and medicinal plants, such as mint, angelica, rhubarb, parsley, wild strawberries, or marsh mallow.

In more shady gardens, plant ferns, dwarf rhododendrons and azaleas – some have a delicious fragrance. These plants need an acid soil rich in peat.

In sunny places plant some irises, globe flowers, cornflowers, rudbeckia, marguerites and forget-me-nots. Make a border with campanula, burnet, lavender or corydalis. You can sow directly into the ground or transplant nigella, marigold, tagetes, cosmos.

Leave the weeds where they are. Plant valerian next to red campion, and foxglove, honesty and verbascum in shady corners.

For the enthusiast.

With your knowledge and painstaking efforts, you will truly be able to master the plants in your garden. You attach a great deal of importance to the overall aesthetic effect. Your choice of flowers can be more sophisticated and you can allow yourself to try your luck by giving your plants rather less than ideal conditions, and compensating them with additional care. So you can become a real experimenter and each new result will fill you with satisfaction.

Sow your own plants, including perennials. It takes a little time, but it is much more fun. Those that survive will be much more robust and better adapted. I once sowed a mixture of geraniums. Each new flower was an exciting surprise.

Keep the seeds of your flowers and have fun growing them. I have a lemon tree that is six years old on my terrace. It grew from a lemon pip planted in a little pot on a windowsill.

Try to recognize the young shoots that spring up among your plants. Replant those that produced pretty flowers next to your perennials.

Sow a little sorrel, cress, parsley and chive. Try to grow little outdoor cyclamens at the foot of trees and gentians at the edge of your borders.

My tips.

In spring I protect young plants by surrounding them with twigs kept for this purpose from winter pruning. They very quickly get lost in the greenery.

I keep a packet of all sizes of bamboo stakes in reserve. I place them next to bushes that spread too much or flower stems that are too supple.

I bought myself a little hand spray that I fill with used dish-washing water plus the filtered juice of cigarette-ends. At the first serious attack of aphids, I spray the plant generously with this mixture which is very effective in getting rid of them.

I always grow three plants of the same sort; the group effect is more attractive. In the event of one of them dying, I can replace it at the end of the season without being deprived in the meantime of that particular type of plant. I have also noticed that plants develop better in a little cluster.

At the beginning of spring, I take cuttings from the pinks that have survived the winter. They multiply very easily in this way. All you need do is to detach the flower heads from the bases and put them in soil in a dry place, watering them occasionally. (Fig. 1)

When my lettuce leaves become hard and bitter, I let them go to seed; they produce such pretty flowers.

The birds have a fine old time all summer in my garden because of the very wide variety of plants at their disposal. I leave a few nettles all year round and I pop catmint in dry places – my garden is a paradise for me as well as for a whole colony of creatures.

FLOWERS AND HERBS

TABLE VI

Perennial flowers.
– with flower spikes
– with flower clusters

Key

	hardy
	crown: spike
	crown: cluster
	slow-growing
	fast-growing
	edible
	scented
I – XII	flowering season

More than 3ft (1m)

Plant	CROWN	GROWTH	EDIBLE	SCENTED	FLOWERING SEASON
Delphinium — *Delphinium belladonna*	spike	fast			VI-VII
Hollyhock — *Althaea rosea*	spike	slow			VIII-IX
Great Mullein — *Verbascum thapsus*	spike	slow			VI-VIII
Horseradish — *Armoracia rusticana*	cluster	fast	edible		V-VI
Foxglove — *Digitalis purpurea*	spike	fast			VI-IX
Goat's Rue — *Galega officinalis*	spike		edible		VII-IX

2½-3ft (0.8-1m)

Plant	CROWN	GROWTH	EDIBLE	SCENTED	FLOWERING SEASON
Bellflower — *Campanula persicifolia*	spike	fast			V-VIII
Viper's Bugloss — *Echium*	spike	slow			VI-IX
Marsh Mallow — *Althaea officinalis*	spike	slow	edible	scented	VII-IX
Monkshood — *Aconitum napellus*	cluster	fast			VI-IX
Bleeding Heart — *Dicentra spectabilis*	cluster	fast			IV-V
Golden Rod — *Solidago*	spike	slow			VII-IX
Obedient Plant — *Physostegia virginiana*	spike	slow			VII-IX
Purple Loosestrife — *Lythrum salicaria*	spike				VI-IX
Prairie Mallow — *Sidalcea malvaeflora*	spike	fast			VI-VIII
Honesty — *Lunaria annua*	cluster	fast			VI-IX

1½-2ft (0.4-0.7m)

Plant	Crown	Growth	Edible	Scented	Flowering Season
Lupin — Lupinus polyphyllus					V-VII
Snapdragon — Antirrhinum majus					VII-X
Tarragon — Artemisia dracunculus					VI-VIII
Catmint — Nepeta cataria					VI-IX
Bellflower — Campanula glomerata					VI-VIII
Vervain — Verbena officinalis					VIII-X
Alkanet — Anchusa officinalis					VI-VIII
Lemon Balm — Melissa officinalis					VII-IX
Snakeweed — Polygonum bistorta					VI-X
Spearmint — Mentha spicata					VII-IX
Common Sorrel — Rumex acetosa					V-VII
Hound's-tongue — Cynoglossum officinale					V-VIII
Yellow Loosestrife — Lysimachia vulgaris					VII-IX

6in-1ft (0.15-0.3m)

Plant	Crown	Growth	Edible	Scented	Flowering Season	Light
Sage — Salvia officinalis					VI-VII	Sun-loving
Monkey Flower — Mimulus gluttatus					VI-IX	Sun-loving
Coral Flower — Heuchera sanguinea					V-VII	Tolerate shade
Heather — Erica					VII-IX	Tolerate shade
Self-heal — Prunella grandiflora					VI-XI	Tolerate shade
Lily-of-the-Valley — Convallaria majalis					IV-V	Tolerate shade
Cowslip — Primula veris					IV-V	Tolerate shade
Ground Ivy — Glechoma hederacea					III-V	Shade-loving
Creeping Jenny — Lysimachia nummularia					VI-VIII	Shade-loving
Lungwort — Pulmonaria officinalis					III-V	Shade-loving
Bugle — Ajuga reptans					IV-V	Shade-loving
Yellow Archangel — Lamiastrum galeobdolon					V-VI	Shade-loving

TABLE VII

Flowers with individual flower-heads or umbels.

Key

	hardy
	individual
	umbel
	slow-growing
	fast-growing
	edible
	scented
I – XII	flowering season

More than 3ft (1m)

	CROWN	GROWTH	EDIBLE	SCENTED	FLOWERING SEASON
Fennel *Foeniculum vulgare*	umbel	✓	✓	✓	VII–IX
Perennial Sunflower *Helianthus decapetalus*	individual	✓	✓		VII–IX
Felwort *Gentiana lutea*	individual				VI–VIII
Angelica *Angelica archangelica*	umbel	✓	✓	✓	VI–IX
Valerian *Valeriana officinalis*	umbel	✓	✓	✓	VI–VIII
Meadow Sweet *Filipendula ulmaria*	umbel	✓	✓	✓	VII–X
Sweet Joe Pye *Eupatorium cannabinum*	umbel	✓			VII–X

2½-3ft (0.8-1m)

	CROWN	GROWTH	EDIBLE	SCENTED	FLOWERING SEASON
Sweet Cicely *Myrrhis odorata*	umbel	✓	✓	✓	IV–VI
Salsify *Tragopogon porrifolius*	individual	✓	✓		IV–VI
Coneflower *Rudbeckia laciniata*	individual	✓			VI–X
Musk Mallow *Malva moschata*	individual	✓	✓	✓	VII–VIII
Japanese Anemone *Anemone hybrida*	individual	✓			VIII–X
Chinese Peony *Paeonia lactiflora*	individual	✓		✓	V–VI
Tansy *Tanacetum vulgare*	umbel	✓			VII–X
Rhubarb *Rheum rhaponticum*	umbel	✓	✓		V–VI
Lovage *Levisticum officinale*	umbel	✓	✓	✓	VI–VII
Oxeye Daisy *Leucanthemum vulgare*	individual	✓			VI–IX
Soapwort *Saponaria officinalis*	individual	✓			VI–IX

1½-2ft (0.4-0.7m) — CROWN · GROWTH · EDIBLE · SCENTED · FLOWERING SEASON

Plant	Edible	Scented	Flowering Season
Perennial Cornflower — *Centaurea montana*			V-VII
Perennial Cornflower — *Centaurea dealbata*			VI-VII
Blue Lettuce — *Lactuca perennis*	edible		V-VIII
Fleabane — *Erigeron speciosus*			VI-VIII
Feverfew — *Tanacetum parthenium*	edible	scented	VI-IX

6in-1ft (0.15-0.3m) — CROWN · GROWTH · EDIBLE · SCENTED · FLOWERING SEASON

Plant	Edible	Scented	Flowering Season
Leopard's Bane — *Doronicum* "Gold Dward"			IV-VI
Alpine Geum — *Geum montarium* / *Geum reptans*			V-VII
Welsh Onion — *Allium fistulosum*	edible	scented	VI-VII
Meadow Crane's-bill — *Geranium pratense*		scented	VI-IX
Perennial Chamomile — *Chamaemelum nobile*	edible	scented	VIII-IX

Sun-loving

Plant	Edible	Scented	Flowering Season
Scabious — *Scabiosa caucasica*			VI-X
Spurge — *Euphorbia polychroma*			IV-V
Columbine — *Aquilegia vulgaris*			V-VI
Globe Flower — *Trollius europaeus*			V-VI
Red Valerian — *Centranthus ruber*			VI-X
Yarrow — *Achillea millefolium*		scented	VI-IX

Plant	Edible	Scented	Flowering Season
Pasque Flower — *Pulsatilla vulgaris*			IV-V
Sweet Violet — *Viola odorata*	edible	scented	II-IV
Sweet Woodruff — *Galium odoratum*	edible	scented	IV-V
Wild Strawberry — *Fragaria vesca*	edible	scented	VI-VII
Navelwort — *Omphalodes verna*			II-V
Primrose — *Primula vulgaris*			III-IV

Tolerate shade

Plant	Edible	Scented	Flowering Season
Sneezewort — *Achillea ptarmica*			V-VIII
Masterwort — *Astrantia major*			VI-VII

Plant	Edible	Scented	Flowering Season
Christmas Rose — *Helleborus niger*			I-III
Lesser Periwinkle — *Vinca minor*			II-V

Shade-loving

TABLE VIII

Perennial rock plants.

Flowering plants – medium height.

Flowering plants – low-growing.

Key

- hardy
- crown: spike
- crown: cluster
- crown: individual flower head
- crown: umbel
- edible
- scented
- I – XII   flowering season

	CROWN	GROWTH	EDIBLE	SCENTED	FLOWERING SEASON
Stonecrop — Sedum rhodiola	umbel	scented			VII-IX
Saxifrage — Saxifraga aizoon	individual	scented			V-VI

	CROWN	GROWTH	EDIBLE	SCENTED	FLOWERING SEASON
Bellflower — Campanula carpatica	spike	scented			XI-IV
Fleabane — Erigeron mucronatus	individual				XI-IV
Bloody Crane's-bill — Geranium sanguineum	individual	scented			XI-V
Rock Rose — Helianthum alpestre	individual	scented			IIV-IV
Rock Cress — Aubretia deltoidea	individual	scented			V-III
Moss Phlox — Phlox subulata	cluster	scented			V-VI
Thrift — Armeria maritima	umbel	scented			IIV-V
Maiden Pink — Dianthus deltoides	individual	scented			XI-IV
Alyssum — Alyssum saxatile	umbel	scented			IV-VI
Rockery Speedwell — Veronica prostrata	spike	scented			IIV-V
Dwarf Flag Iris — Iris pumila	individual	scented			VI-III
Rock Soapwort — Saponaria ocymoides	individual				XI-IIV
Gentian — Gentiana septemfida	individual	scented			IIIV-IIV
Cross Gentian — Gentiana cruciata	individual	scented			XI-IV

Herbs – medium height.

	CROWN	GROWTH	EDIBLE	SCENTED	FLOWERING SEASON
Tarragon *Artemisia dracunculus*					VI-VII
Sage *Salvia officinalis*					VII-VIII
Lavender *Lavandula angustifolia*					VII-VIII
Rosemary *Rosmarinus officinalis*					V-VII
Salad Burnet *Poterium sanguisorba*					V-VII
Chives *Allium Schoenoprasum*					

Herbs – low-growing.

	CROWN	GROWTH	EDIBLE	SCENTED	FLOWERING SEASON
Common Thyme *Thymus vulgaris*					V-VII
English Wild Thyme *Thymus arcticus*					VI-IX
Lemon Thyme *Thymus x citriodorus*					VI-IX
Sweet Marjoram *Origanum majorana*					VI-IX
Hyssop *Hyssopus officinalis*					VI-IX
Parsley *Petroselinum crispum*					
Winter Savory *Satureja montana*					VII-IX

All theses species like full sun and dry soil.

TABLE IX

Plants from bulbs and tubers.

Tall

Plant	Overwinter Indoors	Form	Scented	Flowering Season
Amaryllis		bulb		V-VII
Lilium hansonii		bulb	scented	VI-VII
Dahlia	W	tuber		VII-X
Agapanthus		tuber		VII-VIII

Medium

Plant	Overwinter Indoors	Form	Scented	Flowering Season
Narcissus		bulb	scented	III
Tulip		bulb		III-IV
Iris germanica		rhizome		III-IV
Iris xiphioides		bulb		VI-VII
Iris sibirica		rhizome		VI-VII
Gladiolus	W	bulb		VII-VIII
Dahlia	W	tuber	scented	VII-X
Begonia	W	tuber		VII-XI

Short

Plant	Overwinter Indoors	Form	Scented	Flowering Season
Snowdrop		bulb		II
Crocus		bulb		II-III
Muscari		bulb		IV
Hyacinth		bulb	scented	IV
Iris pumila		rhizome		V
Anemone de Caen	W	tuber		VI-VII
Cyclamen europaeum		tuber	scented	VII-VIII
Colchicum		bulb		X-XI

Key

- bulb — form: bulb
- rhizome — form: rhizome
- tuber — form: tuber
- **W** — store in cellar over winter
- I – XII — months of flowering

TABLE X

Annual plants.

Tall — Sun-loving

Plant	Seed or Plant	Edible	Scented	Flowering Season
Sweet Pea	grow from seed		scented	VI-VII
Nasturtium	grow from seed	edible	scented	VI-X
Morning Glory	grow from seed			VII-XI
Cosmos	grow from seed			VII-XI
Borage	buy as plant	edible		VII-X

Medium

Plant	Seed or Plant	Edible	Scented	Flowering Season
Cumin	buy as plant	edible	scented	VIII-IX
Dill	grow from seed	edible	scented	VIII-X
Pot Marigold	grow from seed		scented	VI-XI
Stocks (Biennial)	grow from seed			III-X
Mignonette	grow from seed		scented	VI-VIII
Opium Poppy	grow from seed			VI-VIII
Cornflower	grow from seed			VII-X
Pinks	buy as plant		scented	VI-XI
Lavatera	buy as plant			VII-X

Short — Sun-loving / Tolerate shade

Plant	Seed or Plant	Edible	Scented	Flowering Season
Basil	buy as plant	edible	scented	VII-X
Summer Savory	grow from seed			VII-XII
Dwarf Nasturtium	grow from seed	edible	scented	VI-XI
Lettuce	grow from seed	edible		
Parsley	buy as plant	edible		
Mesembryanthemum	grow from seed			VI-X
Nemophila	grow from seed			VI-X
Arabis	buy as plant			VI-X
Lobelia	buy as plant			VI-XI
Verbena	buy as plant	edible	scented	VI-XI
Pansy	buy as plant			IV-XI
Garden Cress	grow from seed	edible		
Forget-me-not	grow from seed			IV-V
French Marigold	buy as plant		scented	VI-XI

Sun-loving

Tolerate shade

Key

- hardy
- grow from seed
- buy as plant
- edible
- scented
- – XII flowering season

OUR TERRACES

THE TERRACE, A HANGING GARDEN!

In town, there are almost as many patios as there are gardens. For many city dwellers, they are often the only way of recreating a little corner of nature among the bricks and concrete, while others feel their garden would not be complete without one.

Overlooking the street.

There are the little balconies where you sometimes see a birdcage hanging among the flowerpots: a splash of beauty in a rather dreary street.

There are also the often very large roof-top terraces on top of modern apartment blocks.

Overlooking the garden.

In town, many old houses have a flat-roofed extension which has been or can be converted into a terrace.

They often have a patio at ground level which gives access to the garden.

The terrace, a little corner of the Mediterranean?

For me, this additional small area

of greenery is a Mediterranean botanical garden. It is where I do everything I can't do in the garden, to the great satisfaction of the pair of coal-tits that have taken up residence in the new nest box hanging by my bedroom window.

Terraces, no matter which way they face, usually get more sun than city gardens and you'll find it well worth your while to create a hanging garden. Your efforts will be rewarded the minute the sun comes out. Or after a summer storm, when you'll appreciate the fragrances that are released. And even in winter, terraces are far from dreary places, as the last plants finish flowering in their terracotta pots.

Greenhouse shrubs and plants.

For gardening fanatics, terraces provide quite a considerable extension of the garden, where plants requiring a lot more warmth and light can be grown. The terrace is ideal for greenhouse plants such as mimosa, lemon trees, bay and almond, provided they are brought indoors before the heavy frosts. It is also the perfect spot for various types of geranium and petunias, all kinds of tobacco plants and a whole range of sun-loving annuals and rockery plants.

Your most tender seedlings will do well there and you'll be able to grow all kinds of cuttings.

Beware the heat wave!

With all these advantages there must obviously be a few drawbacks. Your flower-covered patio is entirely at your mercy. A day without being watered during a hot spell will be fatal for some of the more delicate plants. Water evaporates very quickly from a small flower pot. A hanging basket needs, at least, a pint of water a day to keep the plants alive.

So during the summer, you'll be rather tied to your patio. But what a wonderful way to be tied! I have got into the habit of staying in town during the summer, without the slightest longing for the overcrowded roads and beaches. Later on, when my garden is resting, I can go and enjoy nature somewhere else.

How do you convert a flat roof into a terrace?

Several of my friends, who loved the layout of my terraces, asked me how I did it...

First of all, check that there are no regulations, for example in local by-laws, deeds or in your tenancy agreement, which prevent you using the area as a terrace.

Then make sure that the basic structure of the flat roof is solid enough. Old town houses nearly always have a structure of 3 x 7 in (7 x 18cm) wooden beams, 15-18 in (35-45cm) apart, covered with sheets of solid wood, then sheets of roofing felt. This type of structure is as strong as an internal floor and will take the weight of a thin layer of concrete, and the earth-filled containers that you are going to stand on it.

On the other hand, the roofing felt alone will not stand up to frequent use and the weight of tubs of flowers. Do not use the flat roof as it is, or it will soon be damaged and could cause a lot of problems.

A slatted surface.

If you don't own your own home, or you don't want to undertake a large scale job, you can cover the surface of the roof with slats in the form of removable wooden grids. They are very easy to make and you will need between four and six grids, depending on the area of the terrace. (Fig. 1)

Just nail, or better still screw, some solid planks of wood, about the thickness of your thumb and 4 in (10cm) wide, onto batons about 1¼ x 1¼ in (3 x 3cm). You'll need four batons for a grid measuring 4½ ft (1.5m) Leave a space of about ½ in (1cm) between the planks to allow water to run through. (Fig. 2)

Give them a coat of wood preservative or, if you prefer, yacht varnish.

Place the grids next to each other to form a floor. They can easily be removed for cleaning purposes or to check the roofing.

A tiled surface – how to lay it.

Again, take advice in the construction of your roof. Listen to that advice! But the professionals will also tell you that the tiling can't be done. Don't take too much notice. You obviously can't have a

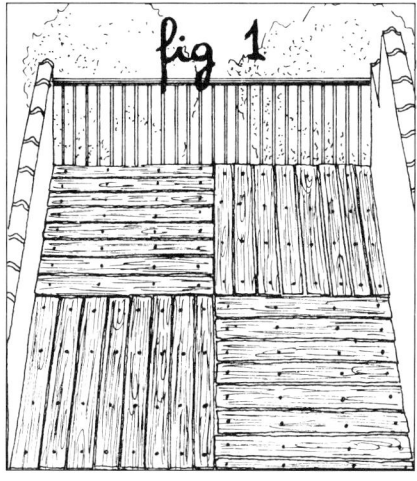

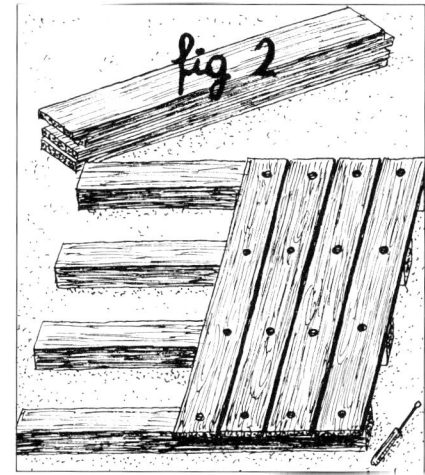

rave up or do the high jump on it, but it wears well under normal conditions. And provided the roof is strong enough, then the worst that can happen is a few cracks in your tiles. First of all check that the roofing felt is watertight.

1. The first step involves covering the entire surface with a single piece of builders' plastic sheeting, allowing it to overlap by 4-6 in (10-15cm) all the way around. The sheeting is sold in various widths at builders' merchants.

2. Next, lay small-mesh chicken wire over the sheeting. You may need two or more strips depending on the size of the terrace. You can buy this in any hardware shop.

3. Place two wooden boards at right angles to the flat surface, at each end of the wire. This will allow you to give the surface the necessary slope, ½ in per yard (1cm per metre), and you can also use them for support when you are smoothing out the cement. Pour a layer of light concrete over the wire (I used a mixture of sand and cement). Add a water repellent in the proportions indicated. The concrete must be at least 1 in (2.5cm) thick at the thinnest points.

4. After a day or two, when the concrete has hardened, you can take the boards away and fill the gaps they've left. Remember to keep the concrete damp. Don't let

it dry out too quickly or it will crack.

5. Finally, after a week, you can lay the tiles, using an adhesive with an added water repellent. Lay them so that they slope evenly down to the guttering, avoiding dips which will collect water.

For one of my terraces, I used old hexagonal terracotta tiles, a good 1 in (2cm) thick. But they proved quite difficult to lay because of their awkward shape, and I had trouble cutting them to the correct dimensions. The finished result, though, is much better and more attractive than on the other terrace where I used thinner, modern tiles designed for the purpose. The first terrace is still intact after two hard winters and it has had a lot more use, whereas the second has cracked slightly across its width, although not seriously.

6. The joints between the tiles on both terraces were filled with white cement mixed with water repellent. Cut off any protruding plastic and carefully re-grout the edges of the terrace.

The most boring job is cleaning the tiles after the joints have been filled. Make sure you rub them down the same day with damp builders' sand to remove all traces of cement. If you fail to do this within a few hours, the job will take you days of work.

The cost of materials for this do-it-yourself job is minimal and the result is extremely pleasing. The irregular shapes of the old tiles give the terrace a Mediterranean look. Terracotta is very pleasant to walk on barefoot in the evening, or after it's rained!

A balustrade!

If your flat roof wasn't intended to be used as a terrace, it won't have a balustrade. For safety you must have one. An airbrick wall or wrought iron fence will do. But make sure it is in keeping with the style of any means of access to

the garden, so that you don't spoil the general appearance of the building.

HOW TO LAY OUT YOUR TERRACE FOR YOUR PLANTS.

Shelving

Nothing could be easier than putting up wooden shelves. All you have to do is fix three right-angle brackets to the wall. On the brackets you place two planks ¾in (2cm) thick by 4in (10cm) wide, leaving a small space between them. As for all external woodwork, give it a coat of wood preservative and repeat this every two or three years. Treated in this way, wood will last for years in all seasons and all kinds of weather conditions. Put various sized pots and containers on the shelves.

Hanging pots and containers.

You will find brackets for your containers in supermarkets and garden shops. Some can be hooked onto a railing, others have to be screwed into position. You can also use them to hang containers from the railing around the edge of your terrace. (Fig. 3)

You can also get wire plant pot holders which you can use to hang pots at different heights. This

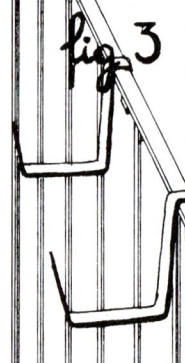

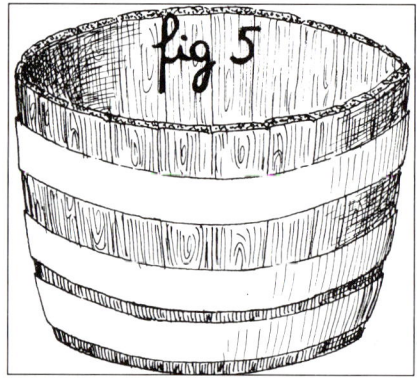

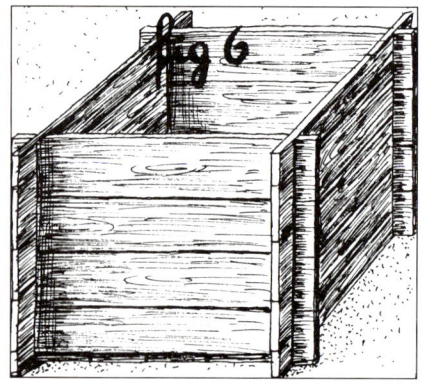

is a good way of brightening up walls. (Fig. 4)

There is also a wide range of stoneware pots available which you can stand on walls.

Free-standing pots for larger plants.

For plants which are going to grow over a period of a few years, for example a climbing plant or a fruit tree, you must choose a container large enough to hold the amount of soil they will need. The pots can be terracotta, or another material, about 18in (45cm) in diameter. You can even use tubs made from half a barrel. (Fig. 5)

You can either buy or make wooden Scandinavian-type containers. They are made from pieces of wood of the same shape which are slotted together, and have the added advantage that you can make them to any height. (Fig. 6) The first two and the last two planks are half width. All the other planks are the same width. (Fig. 7) The base is fitted into a slot in the

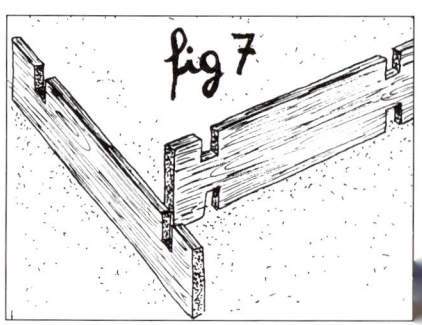

side of the first two half-widths. (Fig. 6)

This last type of container is not very easy to move, so use it for plants that can be left outside during the winter.

Wine crates (the 12 or 24 bottle size) can be used as containers, too. Stand them on wooden blocks to stop the bottom rotting.

Free-standing containers for low-growing plants.

Shallow crates or long containers are ideal. You don't need as much soil to fill them. They can be moved easily and the plants don't dry out as quickly as they do in flowerpots.

I much prefer terracotta and wood to other materials. For reasons best known to themselves, plants do much better in them.

Asbestos will do at a pinch, but plastic containers are terrible. They have no ventilation and the soil becomes acid very quickly. Terracotta containers are quite expensive, but they weather well and last for years.

Perhaps wood does not last as well, but it is still very tough, particularly if it is treated from time to time with wood preservative.

Be sure, though, to use a preservative that is not harmful to plants.

To make your wooden containers last even longer, you can put a layer of gravel or cinders in the bottom which prevents it coming into direct contact with damp soil. If you are keen on do-it-yourself, you will prefer wood as you can cut it to any size you want.

Here are the instructions for an average-size wooden container (Fig. 8):

Length: between 30-45 in (80-1.20m)
Height, 2 planks, about 10 in (25cm)
Width, 2 planks, about 10 in (25cm)

Assemble the planks for the ends first, and then fix the front and back planks on to the thicker uprights. Nail on the bottom and hold it in place with two strips of wood which will also raise it off the ground. (Fig. 9) Make two holes in each end and thread a

piece of thick rope through to use as handles when you want to move the container.

Hanging baskets.

With a little imagination you can create some very original hanging baskets. Mine are made from old, varnished, terracotta plant pot holders of a suitable depth placed in macramé hangers.

The soil in your containers.

Use a mixture of 1/3 soil from the garden, 1/3 leaf compost and 1/3 plant compost with a little organic fertilizer added.

Renew the mixture each spring with about 1/3 new soil. I use my own compost.

At the beginning of the summer I sprinkle a little organic fertilizer on my containers, taking care not to overdo it as it burns the plants.

For evergreen plants, use an organic fertilizer for acid soil, such as a conifer fertilizer.

Look after your containers.

Once or twice during the summer, loosen the surface of the soil in your containers as it quickly forms a crust and won't absorb the water. Although they are being watered, the plants dry out because the water runs down the inside of the pot and out through the holes at the bottom.

I use a small tool, as shown in Fig. 10, or you can use an old fork.

Water the plants on your terrace.

Start to water in spring, when the weather is dry. During spells of drier weather, you must water the plants in your containers regularly every two or three days.

Water every day in hot weather.

Use a small watering can which allows the water to soak slowly into each container and also makes it easier to measure the amount of water you give them. In hot weather, when water evaporates quickly, pots need at least 1 pint (500ml) of water a day and containers need between 4 and 6 pints (2-3l) or more, depending on their size. Remember, water evaporates more quickly from wooden containers.

I never use a rose on the can to water the plants on my terraces. It makes it difficult to judge how much water they have had, which is usually not enough.

If the hot weather lasts for some time, I water the leaves of the plants on my terraces, using a watering can with a rose, after I have watered the plants. This prevents the plants being damaged during a heatwave and they keep their luxuriant green foliage.

Plants that need more water.

Some plants need more water than others. Put the less demanding plants in flowerpots, or stand the flowerpots in pot holders which can be filled with water. Geraniums, thyme, savoury and aubrietia don't need a lot of water, whereas petunias, lobelia and forget-me-nots like sun, but need a lot of water. Sweet peas will dry out in a day if they are not watered.

In winter, never water the plants on your patio.

Plants that need some shade.

Some plants like a sunny position, but also like shade for a few hours during the day, for example, marigolds, begonias, pansies, lavatera.

When arranging your plants, take account of the hours of sunlight in the different parts of the terrace, so that each plant is in the best possible position. You can use larger plants to provide shade for the smaller ones.

When it freezes.

You need somewhere in the house where you can put the plants which don't withstand frost and make sure you bring them in before the hard frosts. Remember, though, that it's warmer in town than in the country. It won't freeze on your patio until the temperature falls to −5°C (23°F), but watch out for your plants when there is an icy wind blowing onto your patio as this will cause a rapid drop in temperature.

Where do you put the delicate plants in winter?

In a light, airy room in the basement, in a conservatory which is not too hot, or on the landing.

They will need very little water during the winter, which is a dormant period for plants. Give them a little water, once a month, or once every two weeks if they are in a heated room.

Some plants which are less vulnerable to frost, can spend the winter on the terrace. A good layer of mulch around their roots will help protect them.

In spring.

As soon as the heavy frosts are over, you can put all the more delicate plants back outside.

Your geraniums will need a good tidying up. Cut them back to a height of about 4 in (10cm) which will force them to send up new growth. You can do this by cutting the stem at a joint and you can replant the cuttings in a light, moist (not wet) soil in a fairly shady spot. You will find they take very easily.

I prefer to lift and replant the geraniums in my containers every spring. I can turn and improve the soil and trim the roots to promote new growth.

Which plants do you put on your terrace?

Annuals and perennials love the sun. And all sun-loving plants which do well in dry soil are ideal for your patio, i.e. all types of geranium, petunia, aubrietia, lobelia, nasturtium, gazania, begonia, ageratum and freesia as well as wallflowers, mignonettes, impatiens, aster and zinnias.

You can buy all these varieties and many others as young plants from your nursery. Alternatively, you can grow them from seed. But for the plants to flower by June, you will need to show the seeds indoors in February or March.

Rock plants.

The terrace is the ideal spot for the scented herbs which grow on dry scrubland. Plants such as sage, savoury, thyme and hyssop will do much better here than in the garden, and will be quite happy to stay on the terrace throughout the winter.

Rosemary is not as resistant to frost, and basil must be brought inside at the first sign of winter, if you want it to last until the following year.

Mediterranean shrubs.

Olive, bay, lemon and rosemary will grow on your terrace, provided they are brought inside during the winter. Eucalyptus, almond and santolina can stay outside if

the winter is not too severe. But take the precaution of protecting their roots with a mulch.

The more delicate shrubs.

Buddleia, winter jasmine, flowering currant, rose bushes and climbing roses will provide shade for your terrace and can stay outside during the winter. Train them

against the walls, using wooden struts and trellis.

Containers for seedlings.

You can use broad, shallow containers for sowing seeds and pricking out seedlings. Afterwards you can fill them with creeping plants which like dry soil and sun, such as mesembryanthemum, with their pale, fragile, daisy-like flowers and fleshy leaves. Alternatively grow plants that you can use in your salads, such as purslane.

Flowering window boxes.

Use several different sorts of small plants around the shrubs and taller plants in your containers, and even in the pots.

In the summer, plant trailing lobelia and ivy-leaf geraniums around the edges so their flowers cascade over the edge of the container. You'll be delighted with the result. And your terrace will be all the more charming.

My suggestions for the idle gardener.

Choose plants which can survive for a few days without being watered. You tend to be rather forgetful!

At the beginning of spring, you will be delighted by the aubrietia cascading from the pots that you forgot about during the winter.

Enjoy your geraniums, they don't need any attention. Plant a few petunia seedlings. You'll only have to do it once as they self-seed year after year.

If you have a sunny enough position, plant some nasturtiums (a little organic fertilizer will help them grow). Plant about eight seeds, in pairs, per container. There is no need to prick them out. The stronger plant of each pair will survive.

You will love the beautiful scent of summer savoury. Once you've planted it, you won't be able to get rid of it, it spreads. It goes well with all plants, even those in the next container. And it can stand not being watered for several days better then most plants. You can also use it to season your food.

For the occasional gardener.

Clematis montana grows particularly well on patios. It can stand not being watered better than some other varieties of clematis. It flowers early and its clusters of flowers will attract birds.

Train ivy up the walls.

Sow annual climbers like nasturtiums, sweet peas and morning glory in your containers. You'll be amazed by the wealth of flowers that will result from very little effort. Once they are planted zinnias, tagetes, asters, marigolds and cornflowers will need no more attention! Mix them with the more commonly-used geraniums, petunias and lobelia.

If you like to see flowers on your terrace early in spring, plant some carefully chosen bulbs, such as tulips and grape hyacinths, in your tubs in September. You can leave them there after they have finished flowering and your summer flowers will take over.

You can make a very pretty hanging basket with some trailing begonias, lobelia and a few sweet peas.

Plant an almond tree in a shady spot. You will be able to enjoy its lovely blossom in spring.

For the enthusiast.

You will enjoy bay trees and lemon trees. Common white jasmine is easy to grow, but doesn't like hard frosts.

Learn how to take cuttings and layer your plants. The terrace is an ideal place for this sort of experiment and your cuttings will give pleasure to a lot of people.

When taking cuttings, I use a "hotbed" which gives me a good head start on the time of year. You can start using it to plant seeds as early as February: see diagram on page 114.

You will need a crate about 2½-3 ft (0.8-1m) square, and 12 in (30cm) high, with a detachable transparent cover. At the end of January, fill the bottom with a layer of fresh horse manure and pack it well down to a depth of 4 in (10cm). On top of this put a layer of compost to a depth of about 6 in (15cm), and finish with a layer of sieved compost.

Once you have prepared the hotbed, leave it for a few days. When it is nice and warm (the manure ferments and heats up the soil), sow your seeds in squares and label them. To keep the soil moist, water it from time to time using a small watering can with a fine rose.

When it is time to sow in the open ground (March, April or May, depending on the type of plant), the plants in the hotbed will already be at the right height for planting out.

Fill your hanging pots and baskets with all types of flowers: a nasturtium with a petunia and a pansy, thyme and campanulas, arabis and a geranium and so on.

My tips.

I get from one terrace to another by means of an old wooden ladder. I leave it permanently in position and attach hanging baskets full of flowers to it in summer.

I use half of an old barrel to collect the rain water from the roof. I have laid it out as an ornamental pond with a few aquatic plants, and three fish spend the winter in it with the help of an aquarium radiator. The excess water runs into a second barrel before going into the water tank. This is a useful reserve for watering the plants on the terrace when they need it, and the local bird population also appreciates the supply of water.

I let some weeds grow where they take root in the flowerpots.

The catchweed goes really well with the geraniums. There is a petunia surrounded by little yellow wood sorrel flowers. The red nettle spills gracefully over the edge of the pot of mimosa with a self-seeded petunia with its enormous reddish-purple velvet trumpets.

A POND IN THE GARDEN

THE FASCINATION OF THE POOL.

We have all, lost deep in our memory, the experience of finding a pool at some time in our lives.

It may have been a forest pool, shaded by tall trees, with its motionless, apparently lifeless, brown water.

Or a pool in open countryside, rustling and buzzing with life, and hidden among wild plants and grasses.

Or it may have been the sort of little pond that you come across at a bend in the path, surrounded

by buttercups at the edge of a water meadow where tadpoles dart among the green duckweed floating on the surface.

It is the stillness of the water that gives these places their charm and fascination.

But ponds and pools are becoming rarer and rarer... In the country, farmers have received grants to drain pools and wetlands, causing a disaster for everything from migrating birds to the rare newt.

In town gardens, ponds used to be a tradition, but have long since ceased to exist. Nowadays, people who do have water in their gardens, tend to try and imitate

the ornamental ponds, designed by eighteenth century architects, or public fountains.

In a natural setting, water is essential for the preservation of the microfauna in the area. But it is even more necessary in towns where the wildlife is dependent on our little islands of greenery.

A pond in the tiniest garden.

With a pond in your garden, you can recapture the charm of your childhood memories. They are easy to make, and not expensive. All you have to do is follow a few simple rules. And the first of these is the most important – that is to make your artificial pond as natural as possible.

This is absolutely essential if you want it to be filled with pond life. So don't use materials which are complicated or costly, or water which has to be renewed.

What is the best position for your pond?

Your pond should be in a sunny part of your garden. The sun is essential for the development of pond life. Try and choose a spot where there aren't too many trees.

When the trees lose their leaves, large quantities will blow into the pond and a large amount of decomposing vegetable matter

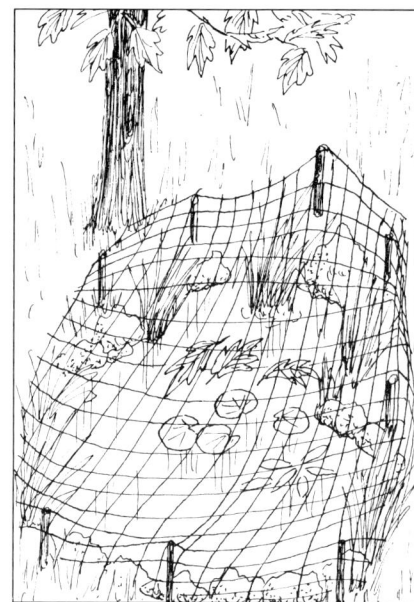

will be a disaster, particularly in the early stages of the development of your pond.

You can cover the pond with a net which will enable you to collect the largest of the falling leaves. Certain types of tree are less harmful than others to pond life, for example conifers and small-leaved trees such as the birch, willow and alder.

Size and shape of your pond.

Your pond can be as big or as small as you want to make it. As an example, let's take a pond of 6 sq ft (2 sq m), which can be constructed perfectly easily in any

fig 1

small town garden, and consider how to build it and set it out.

Never make it deeper than 18 in (50cm), the ideal depth for the development of aquatic plants and to establish a good biological balance.

Dig your pond to an even depth of 18 in (50cm), sloping the edges slightly. This will give it the maximum volume. The amount of water is important, as it will be less likely to dry up during hot spells.

If, as you dig the pool, you come across obstacles that are difficult to get round, such as large stones or tree roots, don't worry. The bottom of your pond can follow the structure of the subsoil. What you must do as you dig, is to make sure that the edges of the pond are all the same level. (Fig. 1)

Make your little pool the shape you want it: round, oval, kidney-shaped or more irregular. Again, the important thing is to avoid making it look artificial. (Fig. 2)

How do you make your pond watertight?

Once you have finished digging the pond, you need to fit a polythene or P.V.C. liner.

Although this is cheap and quick to use, it has one drawback. It is relatively fragile. A sharp object falling into the pond may only make a very small hole, but the water will drain away. I don't need to draw a diagram to point out the problems that this would cause. Your bath runs the risk of being in permanent use for some time!

However, in a quiet and peaceful environment, this method is attractive because it is so simple.

And you can certainly protect your polythene sheeting by laying old rubber-backed carpet underneath (and on top if you like). Alternatively you can cover the polythene sheeting with a 1 in (2.5cm) layer of sand. At least this will stop stones that are trapped underneath from piercing the sheet.

Polythene sheeting is available from builders' merchants in different sizes. Choose one most suitable for the size of your pond, allowing for an overlap of 12-16 in (30-40cm) all the way around the edge. (Fig. 3 below)

Spread the sheeting over the bottom of the pond without worrying about wrinkles.

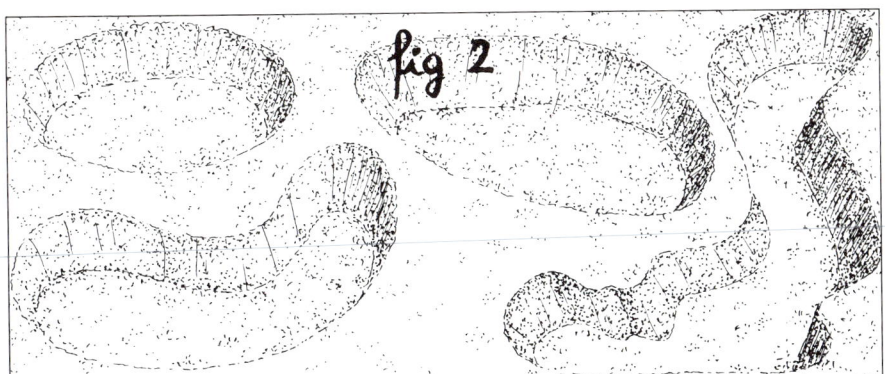

fig 2

Dig out a hollow around the edge of the pond to a depth of between 8-16 in (20-40cm). (Fig. 3) It will soak up the overflow from your pond, and you can fill it with marsh plants.

To hold the sheeting in place, simply cover it with the earth you have dug out. Here and there, you can secure it with a few large stones.

At one point around the edge, leave a flat surface and cover it with flat stones so that the creatures visiting your pond can get in and out. From this point construct a gentle slope into the pond by planting aquatic plants at different depths. (Fig. 3)

A concrete pond is not only more expensive, but you will also have to line it with polyester. Concrete is not very good for the development of pond life as it modifies the pH (acidity) of the water.

Pre-fabricated pools are both expensive and difficult to install, and you won't have the marshy area around the edge. And because of the steep sides you will find hedgehogs and other creatures drowned in your pond.

What sort of water for your pond?

Now your pond is finished, all you have to do is fill it with water.

In theory, rainwater, of which we have a plentiful supply, should be quite suitable for your pond. How-ever, some areas have an acid rainfall, which could mean you are unable to grow aquatic plants. And don't use water from the roof if your guttering is made of lead or asbestos as it will poison the water. You can avoid this by coating the inside of your gutters with a waterproof sealant, such as "Aquaseal", so that the water is safe to use.

Only use rainwater from a tank if the tank is used regularly. Stagnant water must never be used.

When all is said and done, you can use tap water: it is the simplest way of filling your pond. Any chlorine it contains will evaporate in a few days. If you want it to become organic in a short space of time, all you have to do is take a bucket or two of mud and water from a healthy pool and add it to your water.

Evaporation.

In hot weather, your pond will evaporate at the rate of ½ in (1cm) per day. If it has a small surface area, it is important to make sure that the water level is maintained so that the plants around the edge do not dry out. You can buy special taps which maintain a constant water level. You can also have a rainwater reservoir near the pond.

Overflow.

After heavy rain, your pond will overflow but this won't matter if you have created a marshy area around the edge. The marsh plants will be all the better for it.

How do you empty and look after your pond?

You should never empty your pond. So, there is no need to provide a system for emptying it. If, after a while, too much waste matter collects on the bottom, simply remove some of it. The least damaging way is to clear out a maximum of a third of your water and waste at one time.

As for the rest, the aquatic plants will see to it that your pond is kept healthy. When they start to overrun the pond, all you have to do is skim the surface to remove any surplus. The golden rule for the stocking of your pond must be: *always maintain a ratio of one third plants to two thirds water.*

What do you plant in your pond?

All aquatic plants are planted between May and the end of September.

Some varieties are planted on the bottom of the pond, while others are simply thrown into the water where they root, or float on the surface.

Aquatic plants can usually be divided into four categories:

A. submerged plants;
B. floating plants;
C. ornamental plants that are planted on the bottom;
D. marsh plants.

Submerged oxygenating plants to keep your pond clean.

These oxygenating plants are particularly useful for maintaining the quality of the water in your pond. Overall, Lagarosiphon major and Ceratophyllum demersum (hornwort) are the most effective oxygenators, and Myriophyllum proserpinacoides (parrot feather), although not hardy, is excellent for reducing algae in newly-planted ponds. Other plants flower on the surface. You will find a dozen or so of these listed in Table XI.

All you have to do is throw them into the water and they will root.

Floating plants.

These plants are most often seen on the surface of natural pools. The most common, with its characteristic little green discs, is duckweed (Lemna). The water chestnut (Trapa natans) is one of the most attractive floating plants. All floating plants establish themselves and all you have to do is throw a few into the pond. They grow very quickly and will take over if you are not careful. Keep an eye on them and remove the surplus according to the one-third plants, two-thirds water rule.

as their names suggest: Pygmaea alba, rubra and helvola.

Apart from water lilies, there are many other delightful varieties of aquatic plant. You will find a list, which is not exhaustive, in column 3 of <u>Table XI</u> on page 106, but here are a few examples:

Iris laevigata is a large iris, about 2 ft (60cm) high, with blue flowers and white and green variagated foliage.

Acorus gramineus is a smaller, evergreen iris, which grows to a height of between 8-10 in (20-25cm).

Aponogeton distachyus (water hawthorn) spreads across the water in pairs of little white scented flowers between April and May, and then again between September and October. It thrives in very small ponds.

Butomus umbellatus (flowering rush) has clusters of pink flowers during late summer.

Calla palustris (bog arum) grows to a height of between 6-8 in (15-20cm) and is very popular with water snails. In summer it has large white flowers. These are followed by red berries which are poisonous to human beings. (Make sure you plant it out of reach of children!)

Caltha palustris (marsh marigold) is like a buttercup.

Iris palustris (marsh iris) grows in the marshy area around the pond. There are several different varieties, the most common of which is the Iris pseudacorus (yellow flag).

Finally, Scirpus lacustris (the great bulrush) grows in impressive clumps.

Marsh plants.

There are many species in this category which have already been mentioned in the chapter dealing with flowers, for example, carpet bugle, thoroughwort, meadow sweet, astilbe, siberian iris, marsh lobelia and globe flower. In addition, there are the many varieties of hosta and primula.

All these plants grow particularly well in a damp, shady spot. Choose a selection to plant around the edge of your pond where they are kept damp by water soaked up by the soil and any that overflows from the pond.

The plants for your pond.

To help you choose, <u>Table XI</u> presents a selection of plants from each of the four categories. I

Ornamental plants, planted on the bottom.

It is these plants which are particularly pleasing to the eye and have the most attractive flowers. The best-known is the water lily. You will find many varieties at nurseries specializing in aquatic plants.

A very simple way to acquire these is to take a shoot from a parent plant in a natural pool or from a friend's pool.

It is important to remember that all these ornamental plants must be planted at a depth which suits

the individual plant. Otherwise, all you have to do is make sure you plant them between May and the end of September.

There are certain types of water lily which are best suited to large ponds as they cover a large area. Other types, which cover an area of between 12-20 sq in (30-50 sq cm), are more suitable for small ponds. There are also miniature water lilies which are ideal for ponds where the surface is between 2-8 in (5-20cm) below the level of the garden. These are available in white, red and yellow, selected them on the basis of a small pool 6 sq ft (2 sq m) and have given one variety for each of the species mentioned. There is, of course, a much wider range than I have been able to give here.

The table gives you the correct planting depth, the height of the plant above water level and the flowering season.

Where do you get your plants?

There are nurseries which specialize in garden ponds, where there are qualified staff who can advise you.

Aquatic plants are sometimes available in garden supermarkets during May. They probably won't have any specialist staff, so make sure you know what plant you want before you go.

Another way is to get your plants from friends. You can either carefully detach a few cuttings or shoots of the required plant or ask

for a clump when they are dividing their plants.

How do you plant?

The arrangement of your ornamental plants creates the different levels which will give your pond a gentle slope. A slope of this kind is essential as it allows the small creatures that will visit your pond to get into the water.

So for one side of your pond choose plants which are graded gradually according to their planting depth, from 0-20 in (0-50cm). (see Fig. 5)

What do you put your plants in?

Use all sizes of containers for your ornamental plants. This will give you better control over the growth of the roots and will make it easier to contain the vegetation in the pond. You can use anything suitable that allows for the rate at which the plant grows and its planting depth. Old earthenware, iron or plastic pots, hollow logs, brick containers etc. Fill them with special compost and place them so that you provide the planting depth appropriate for each plant.

If the pots are not tall enough, you can raise them with flat stones, tiles, bricks or inverted pots.

To form a continuous slope, fill the gaps between the various

containers with gravel. This will also hold the containers firmly in place. (Fig. 5)

The slopes of the other banks of the pool need not be so regular. Arrange your plants here to produce the desired visual effect.

Which compost do you use?

The soil in which you plant your aquatic plants should be as stable as possible. It takes years for an ordinary compost to develop the

1. Aponogeton distachyus
2. Nymphaea pygmea
3. Iris laevigata
4. Acorus gramineus
5. Butomus umbellatus
6. Iris pseudacorus

necessary properties.

You will find the right sort of compost at a nursery that specializes in aquatic plants.

Another solution is to get it from a well-established, natural pool ake sure it is healthy and not fed ⌐ a polluted water supply. A ⌐odland pool which has its ⌐urce in the same wood would ⌐ ideal.

Failing this, use well-washed ⌐uilders' sand.

⌐hat sort of animal life?

⌐sually, once your pool is finished ⌐d well-stocked with plants, it ⌐ll automatically begin to attract ⌐eatures which live in or near ⌐ater. This will happen gradually.

Insects will probably be the first ⌐ arrive, the others will follow.

But here, in the city?

That won't stop the insects. As far as amphibians are concerned, I am obviously not going to tell you to go hunting for frogs, as they are already an endangered species.

However, there is no reason why you can't keep frogs, even in a town garden, as long as the area in which they will be living is full of the plant and animal life they need. It would be interesting to provide several ponds in one district of a town, with connecting passages under the walls so that

they could extend their territory. A pair of frogs needs an area of 50 sq yds (50 sq m).

Lizards are no respectors of boundaries. It can't be that long since they disappeared from our gardens which were becoming too uncomfortable for them. You may also find that some newts find their way to your pond.

If you inherit a pair of poor homeless toads, fair enough. One of my friends adopted two baby frogs. They have been living in her garden and pond in the middle of town for several years.

You can also try bringing back some tadpoles in some pond water from one of your country walks. With a bit of luck, you will be contributing to the preservation of an endangered species.

Do this when your pond is full of insects and plants. Small amphibians feed on insects and

don't need artificial food.

What sort of fish?

You can put fish in your pond, but not just any variety. Choose hardy species which don't eat plants and are not predatory. The Koi carp is ideal. It grows in proportion to the pond and lives for more than 150 years. It will be able to tell your great-grandchildren the story of your pond! If you feed it at the same time every day, you can train it to eat out of your hand.

It will winter happily in the pond as long as there is some mud at the bottom. Even if the water freezes, the mud won't. The main danger is suffocation. To avoid such a tragedy, make sure that air can get through the ice. Never try and break the ice by hitting it with a blunt instrument. This could concuss or even kill the fish. There are electric heaters, which run on very little current, that will keep an area free of ice.

Only feed your fish between June 1 and September 30. They hibernate for the rest of the year and make do with what there is in the pond.

Don't put more than a total of 6 in (15cm) length of fish for every square foot (0.09 sq m) of surface area in a pond.

When do you put the fish in?

Wait until the plants are well established before you put fish into your

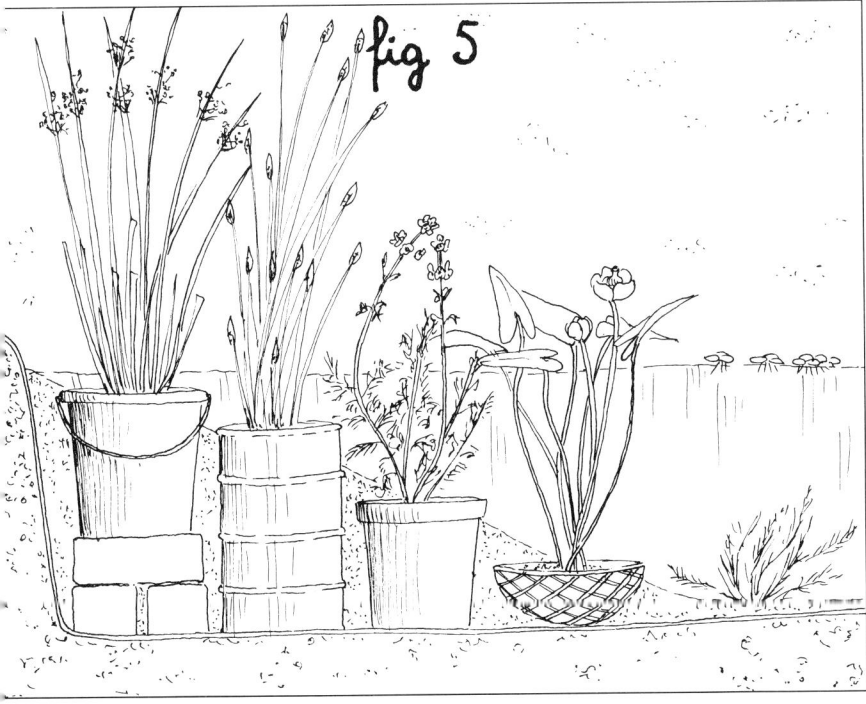

fig 5

pond. If you don't, the fish will up-root the plants, which then won't be able to function properly and the pond will go green.

Algae

There are various types of algae, but the most troublesome are the free-floating and filamentous kinds.

The best way to control the growth of algae is to make sure you have the correct proportion of plants and scavengers for the size of your pond. To keep the water clear, you need one bunch of oxygenating plant for every 2 sq ft (0.18 sq m) of surface area. In addition about one-third of the surface area needs to be shaded with floating plants and lily pads. This will cut down the amount of sunlight reaching the water, making it difficult for the algae to grow.

Both aquatic snails and mussels live on algae and these, too, will help to control its growth. But not all aquatic snails are suitable, because some species will eat your plants as well. The one to recommend is the ramshorn snail which feeds only on algae – mainly the filamentous kind – and won't touch your ornamental plants.

Two species of freshwater mussel are commonly available – the swan mussel and the painter's mussel – and these will eat vast amounts of the free-floating kind of algae.

Aquatic snails and mussel thrive on mature water, so wait while before introducing them into your pond. Mussels also need covering of organic mater at the bottom of the pond to shuffle around in.

By making sure you maintain the natural balance of your pond you can effectively control the growth of algae.

My suggestions for the idle gardener.

Don't think that a pond is not for you. Once it is set out, a pond takes care of itself. Aquatic plants are a lot more obliging and prolific than other varieties. A small pond will add a note of irresistible charm to your garden.

But, if you don't want to spend too much time building a pond, get hold of half an old barrel and put it in the warmest corner of the garden. A few large stones, a clump of water crowfoot and water forget-me-not, a few stems of water milfoil, and you have an instant and extremely delightful pond. Don't forget the goldfish, a shubunkin for example. It is easier to bring it indoors in winter where it will hibernate quite happily in a bowl or even in a bucket.

For the occasional gardener.

Choose the quickest and easiest method, a piece of polythene sheeting held in place with some large stones. Or simpler still, a raised pond, between railway sleepers. Surround it with purple loosestrife, comfrey, meadow sweet and various sorts of iris. For the bottom of your pond use some pre-washed builders' sand and a few stones from a river bed. Plant a white water lily which has medicinal properties, some marsh marigold and flowering rush.

A few veiltails will add life to your pond.

For the enthusiast.

If you have the space, don't hesitate, build the biggest pond you can using plastic sheeting. Put a layer of soft felt or sand underneath it. This will make it more hardwearing. Use marginal plants around the edges of your pond to create a natural effect. A layer of vegetation will spring up, water forget-me-not, water crowfoot, duckweed, and the edges of the pond will blend with the surface of the garden.

If you are clever, install a little waterfall. It will improve the oxygenation of the water, and you'll love the sound of the water!

My tips.

Wait for at least three or four weeks after putting the plants in your pond before you put in the fish. There may be some initial chemical reactions, especially in wine barrels, which are sometimes quite strong, and these will kill the fish.

To introduce the fish into the pond, put them in a plastic bag containing water, and lay it on the surface of the pond. Leave them for half an hour so that they get used to their new surroundings and then all you have to do is let them out of the bag. It is better to do this after sunset.

I hardly feed the fish. The natural food they find in the pond is enough.

In winter, when it freezes, it is important to maintain a supply of air to the pond. Place a pan full of boiling water on the ice covering the pond. This will make a hole immediately. Then pump out some of the water to create a layer of air under the ice which prevents it reforming. Check the pond every two days. Clear any snow from the ice, as pond life needs light.

You can buy plastic covers which you can place over the pond in winter.

At the end of the summer, I tidy up and divide the aquatic plants which have become too invasive. I give what I don't want to my friends which encourages them to create their own little pool.

You can also exchange plants which enables you to extend your own collection.

TABLE XI

Aquatic and marsh plants.

Key

- type: foliage
- type: foliage
- type: individual flower
- umbel
- cluster
- flower spike or grass

height in inches
above water
(multiply by 2.54 for cm)

planting depth
in inches
(multiply by 2.54 for cm)

M = Marsh

B = Bog

W = Waterside

I-XII Best time of year

Submerged oxygenators and cleaners.

	TYPE	HEIGHT	BEST TIME OF YEAR
Ceratophyllum demersum	foliage		
Elodea canadensis	foliage		V-VIII
Hottonia palustris	foliage	4-12	V-VI
Myriophyllum proserpinacoides	foliage		VII
Myriophyllum spitacum	foliage	1-4	VII
Potamogeton crispus	foliage	1-2½	VI-VIII
Potamogeton perfoliatus	foliage	1-2½	VI-VIII
Ranunculus aquatilis	flower	¾-1	IV-VII
Stratiotes aloides	flower	¾-2	VI-X

Floating.

	TYPE	HEIGHT	BEST TIME OF YEAR
Azolla caroliniana			IX-XII
Hydrocharis morsus ranae	foliage	¾-2	VI-IX
Lemna gibba	foliage		V-XI
Lemna minor	foliage		VII-XI
Lemna polyrhiza	foliage		VII-XI

Simply throw submerged and floating plants into the water and they will "root".

Ornamental.

Plant	TYPE	HEIGHT	DEPTH	BEST TIME OF YEAR
Acorus calamus		80/100	10/35	VI-VII
Acorus gramineus		20/25		VI-VII
Aponogeton dystachyus		1/5	15/50	III-V
Butomus umbellatus		50/60	5/30	VII-XI
Calla palustris		20/40	5/10	V-IX
Caltha palustris		20/50	5/20	III-VI
Equisetum fluviatile		40/80	0/5	I-XII
Iris pseudoacorus		50/100	10/50	IV-VI
Mentha aquatica		30/80	10/50	VII-IX
Myosotis palustris		10/30	0/10	VI-X
Hippuris vulgaris		3/5	20/40	V-VIII
Nuphar lutea		10/30	40/....	VI-X
Polygonum amphibium		5/10	5/30	VII-X
Pontederia cordata		50/60	5/30	VII-X
Ranunculus flammula		20/40	30/50	VII-IX
Sagittaria sagittifolia		40/60	30/50	VI-IX
Scirpus lacustris		100/250	10/50	VI-X
Stachys palustris		20/80	5/15	VI-X
Veronica beccabunga		30/60	10/30	V-IX
Nymphaea		2/3	10/15	VI-X
– Pygmaea alba				
– Pygmaea rubra				
– Pygmaea helveola				
Nymphoides peltata		3/10	20/40	VII-VIII

Waterside and marsh.

Plant	TYPE	HEIGHT	DEPTH		BEST TIME OF YEAR	
Aruncus sylvester		100/150	B	40-60	W	VI-X
Eupatorium atropurpureum		80/100	B	30-40	W	VIII
Eupatorium purpureum		60/100	M	24-40	M	VII-X
Filipendula rubra		120/200	0/–1	48-80	W	VII-IX
Hemerocallis		60/90	B	24-36	W	VI-IX
Hosta		30/90	B	12-36	W	VII-IX
Houttuynia cordata		10/30	B	4-12	W	VI-IX
Iris chrysographes		60/80	B	24-30	W	VI-VII
Iris foetidissima		30/50	B	12-20	W	IX-XI
Iris kaemferi		50/80	B	20-30	W	VI-VII
Iris sibirica		40/80	B	15-30	W	VI-VIII
Lobelia cardinalis		50/70	0/–1	20-28	W	VII-X
Lyschitum americanum		60/90	T	24-36		IV-V
Osmunda regalis (fern)		150/200	M	60-80	M	VI-X
Peltiphyllum peltatum		60/80	T	24-30	B	IV-V
Petasites hybridus		40/80	T	15-30	B	III-V
Physostegia virginiana		40/80	T	15-30	B	III-V
Primula bulleyana		10/30	T	4-12	B	IV-V
Primula beesiana		10/30	T	4-12	B	V-VI
Primula japonica		60/100	0/–1	24-40	0-½	IV-VI
Rheum palmatum atrosanguinea		250/300	0/–1	100-120	0-½	VII-X
Rodgersia podophylla		40/60	0/–1	15-24	0-½	V-VII
Trollius europaeus		30/80	0/–1	12-30	W	VI-VIII
Carex vesicaria		10/20	M	4-8	M	VI-VII
Miscanthus sinensis		120/180	M	48-70	M	VI-VII
Sasa pumila		20/60	M	8-24	M	

PRUNING. A SECRET ART?

Pruning has the reputation of being a difficult art to master. Gardening manuals give lengthy, detailed descriptions of the different aspects and various methods of pruning. There are as many different ways of pruning as there are "pruning experts".

I am obviously not going to try and explain all the various principles here. What I am going to do is to give you a few simple instructions so that you can cope with the basics. The rest depends on individual taste and is a matter of practice and experience.

Three types of pruning: two main types and one subsidiary type.

Shaping saplings
- *Standards.*
- *Espaliers.*

Pruning for fruiting.
- *Summer.*
- *Winter.*

Pruning dead or excess wood.

Before you start, a diagram will help to explain the correct way to remove a twig or small branch.

Make sure you always use well-sharpened secateurs.

Make the cut at an angle, with the lower edge of the secateurs level with the base of the bud, the upper edge level with the top of the bud. (Fig. 1)

Always cut above an outer bud so that the shoot grows outward. This will open up the tree. (Fig. 2)

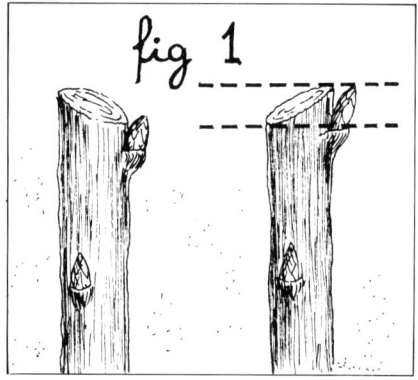

Shaping young standard trees.

The shaping of young standard trees is particularly useful for fruit

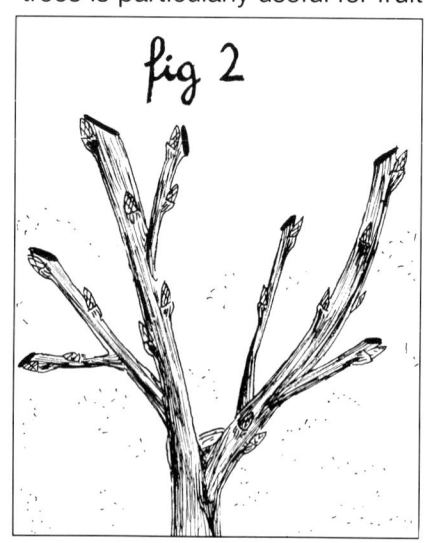

trees. It strengthens the main branches and forces them to open up the crown.

Stone-fruit trees, particularly the cherry, are pruned in summer. This avoids them being affected by gummosis, which is the result of the scar not healing properly.

Apple trees, pear trees and currant bushes are pruned at the end of winter, before the buds open, but no later than March 15.

A year after they have been planted, cut back the three or four main branches to half their length, above an external bud. (Fig. 3)

You do the same thing for the next two years on all new growth which has formed from the point of the previous year's pruning. (Figs. 4 and 5)

Except for cherry trees, which must be strong because of their height, this pruning is not absolutely necessary for stone-fruit trees. Peach, in particular, is much more attractive when left to develop naturally.

Shaping trees to make espaliers.

Pruning is a little different for espaliers because the aim is to enable them to develop three or four main branches on either side of the trunk.

The shaping of young standard trees over a period of three years. Figs. 3, 4 and 5 show the successive stages carried out over three consecutive winters.

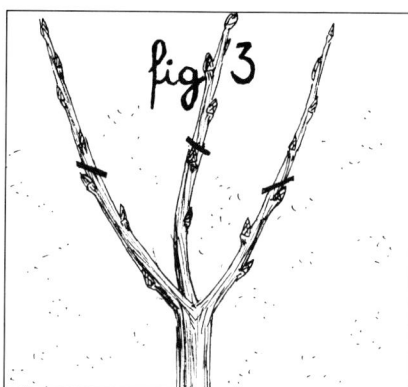

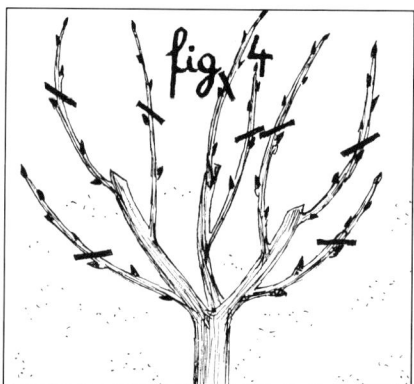

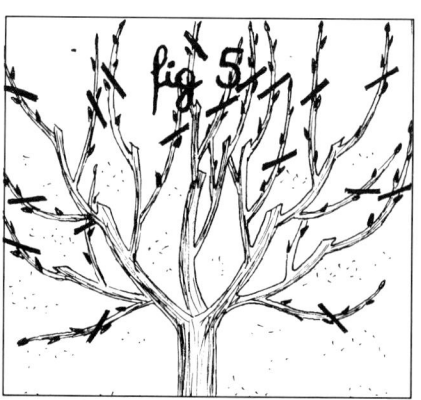

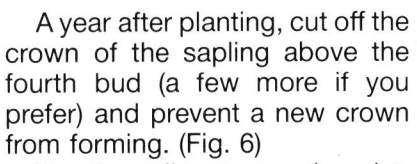

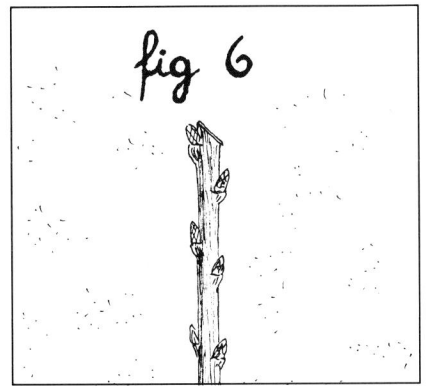

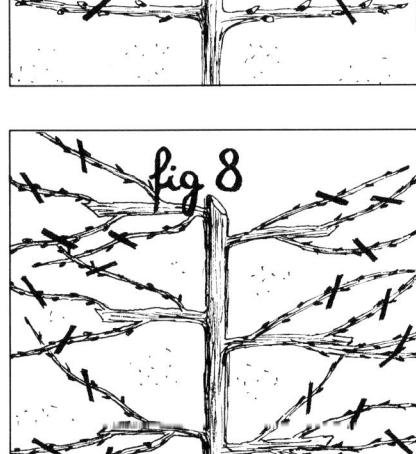

A year after planting, cut off the crown of the sapling above the fourth bud (a few more if you prefer) and prevent a new crown from forming. (Fig. 6)

You then allow two or three lateral branches to develop on each side, cutting them back to half their length for the next two years. (Figs. 7 and 8)

Once the branches have formed, you can train them to suit your individual taste.

Pruning your trees for fruiting.

This only affects each year's new growth, that is the wood that is still green.

You will find this type of pruning particularly useful for pear trees, apple trees and currant bushes.

June or summer pruning for your fruit trees.

1. Get rid of all the suckers. These are the branches that grow more vigorously than the others and which grow straight up. Cut them off at the base. (Fig. 9)
2. Summer pruning. In June, when new growth is strong, cut the shoots back to half their length. (Fig. 9)

For vines: cut back all shoots to above the second leaf after each bunch of grapes.

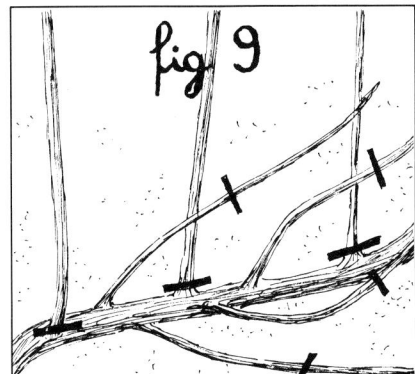

Winter pruning for your fruit trees.

1. Finish the summer pruning on the terminal shoots by cutting them back to two buds. (Fig. 10)
2. Prune the spur-bearing branches. These are the branches that grow from the main branches and support the year's new growth which must be pruned.

I cut them back to above one or two buds, except for those bearing a fruit spur (Fig. 10) or for those bearing a flower bud.

I cut back the new growth to above the first flower bud on growth ending in a flower bud (Fig. 10) and on sprigs: short, slender shoots (Fig. 10) which are more likely to flower and bear fruit.

Winter pruning for your vines.

Keep a single stem of the length you require. At the end of the winter, when the frosts are over, cut back all the new shoots along the length of the stem to two buds.(Fig. 11, p.112) Cut back the growth of the main stem by half.

Pruning your ornamental bushes.

As ornamental bushes begin to grow, I give them an initial pruning to open them up, as I do for the trees. (see Fig. 3)

At the end of the spring when they have finished flowering, I cut

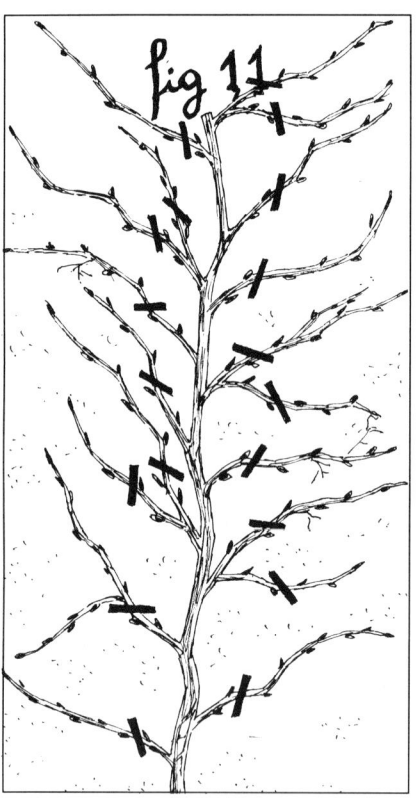

them back to the desired height and width.

I take off all the shoots at the base, except those that will replace some of the branches.

Pruning your hedges.

As they begin to grow, pinch out the head of the saplings (the young plants) to make the shoots grow out to the side. (Fig. 12)

Then cut back the side shoots regularly to allow them to fill out. (Fig. 13)

Pruning dead wood and intersecting branches.

This is done to increase the ventilation of the crown of the tree.

Dead wood can occur at any time of the year, but is more easily identified during summer.

When intersecting branches need pruning, it is better to do this

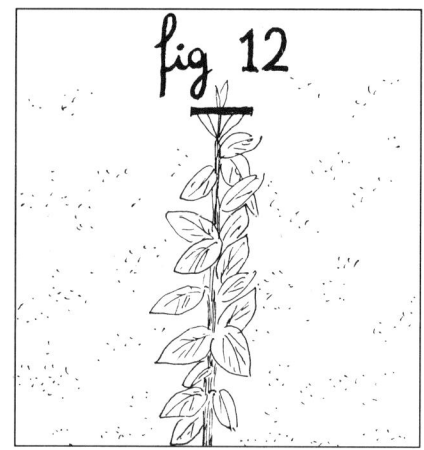

in summer for the stone-fruit trees, and in winter for all the others.

When two branches intersect, I keep the one which shows more potential either in terms of direction or growth. I cut back the other completely or partially if possible. Of course, there's nothing wrong in leaving well alone unless the intersecting branches will interfere with sunlight to the leaves.

GARDEN MAINTENANCE.

To garden efficiently, you don't have to buy a lot of expensive or complicated equipment. All you need are a few basic, sturdy tools, so it's a good idea to avoid being over-influenced by television adverts or the new-fangled gadgets in the garden stores.

What equipment do you need for your flower-beds?

A medium-sized spade with a T-shaped handle is needed for breaking down and turning the soil over.

A hoe or small fork is essential. I prefer the simple triangular-shaped hoe – this is used for loosening the soil in the flower-beds.

Another useful tool is a flat-pronged fork, used for lifting clumps of parent plants, moving

compost and aerating the lawn.

A medium-sized rake, used for raking newly-dug soil and after sowing seeds, is a help. It can also be used for raking areas of gravel or gravel pathways.

What equipment do you need for plants?

A trowel is a must. Make sure it is good quality. It is used for making holes for plants with a root ball, loosening the soil in small areas, filling pots and a host of other general gardening jobs.

In addition you'll need a dibber for pricking out young plants, a tool or a fork for scraping out pots and a small hand spray for spraying soapy water and for spraying young plants.

I often use raffia and various sized stakes for supporting plants and I always have a handy supply of plastic labels and an indelible marker.

Finally, keep a supply of cinders to keep caterpillars at bay.

What equipment do you need for your trees?

I advise you to have an eight-rung step ladder, a pair of absolutely top quality secateurs and a pair of long-handled secateurs if you have old, tall trees.

Smaller useful equipment to make tree-care easier includes plastic ties for the branches, bamboo canes for the espaliers and a large spray pump if you have several fruit trees. This will come in handy when you spray them with a winter tar oil wash.

I rely on a pair of cotton gloves, plus the toughest possible old leather gloves as protection against the thorns when I am trimming bushes.

What equipment do you need for hedge care?

Once you've planted your hedge, you need only a pair of top quality shears for trimming and tough garden gloves to protect your hands if you have thorny plants.

What equipment do you need for your lawn?

A standard lawn mower is all you need if you only have a small area of grass; the simplest model will be adequate.

If you have moss or an area of lawn that regularly gets trodden down you'll need a lawn aerator. You can use the garden fork if you have a very small area of lawn.

Finally, you'll need a grass rake for collecting grass cuttings and leaves. I prefer a bamboo rake.

What do you need for watering the patio and the pots?

To make things easier, keep a small plastic watering can on each floor of the house. In addition keep one or two extra large watering cans for the patio and the garden.

It's essential, also, to have one or two narrow-necked watering cans with a detachable rose.

What are the essentials for watering the garden?

You'll need a hose-pipe on a frame with an adjustable nozzle. It is also particularly useful to have a rain-water tank with an electric pump. It saves an awful lot of water, and, more importantly, rainwater doesn't contain chlorine!

What else do you need for general maintenance and fruit picking?

Small essential items include a sturdy pocket knife, a pair of galoshes or boots, a large, strong wicker basket, a sieve for sieving the soil, old wooden crates, old buckets and a hook for attaching a bucket to the ladders.

Large items include a handcart or wheelbarrow plus a double ladder, with two 10ft (3m) sections, which can be stored outside.

CALENDAR OF THE MAIN MAINTENANCE JOBS IN THE GARDEN.

Autumn.

Fruit picking: Pick winter apples and pears before they become too ripe. Lay them out carefully in the shed on racks or in fruit crates stacked one on top of the other.

Tidying up the garden: Remove the dead branches of plants which have finished flowering and add to the compost heap. Give the lawn its final cut and go over it with the lawn aerator.

Clear up the dead leaves on the

lawn and add to the compost heap. The dead leaves which have fallen on the flower-beds can be left, as they provide protection for the plants during the winter.

Planting: After November 25, plant any new perennials which will flower next summer.

Plant more bulbs – narcissi, tulips, grape hyacinths etc. And now is the time to order your seeds for spring.

Winter.

Remember the birds: During periods of heavy frost and snow, put out water and seed for the garden birds. Tits are fond of monkey nuts and coconut. Make strings of monkey nuts and drill a hole in a coconut, about 1½in (3.5cm), which is big enough for them to get inside. Hang them in a tree. You can also put a little bird table out of reach of cats, where you can put out seed, oat flakes, dried fruit, fat etc.

Spray your fruit trees: when they have stopped growing and the weather is dry and not too cold. Spray the fruit trees with a tar oil wash solution. Later, just before the buds swell, give them a second spraying with an oily product.

These natural products will noticeably reduce attacks by predators and disease the following season, and they are not harmful to the environment.

Prune your fruit trees: Between February and March, prune fruit trees, bushes, currant bushes and vines. Remove dead wood from raspberry canes and tie up the new shoots.

Remove dead wood and unnecessary branches from trees. Keep the twigs for protecting your young plants in spring. This is also a good time to cut back ivy if

necessary.

Repair and maintenance of equipment: Make the most of winter to carry out any necessary repairs to your walls. This dormant period is an ideal time to make new wooden containers and to give the old ones a coat of wood preservative.

Actually in the garden, "springcleaning" is out of the question. Winter is the time for all cleaning – from your nest boxes to your full range of garden tools.

Sow your seeds in the cold frame: Sow your seeds in small trays indoors where there is plenty of light. Prepare your hotbed at the beginning of February.

Spring.

Attend to perennials: As soon as winter is over, divide clumps which have spread too far. Loosen the soil between the plants which are beginning to come through.

Keep an eye out for slugs. Put a used plastic bottle with the bottom cut off, or ashes, around young plants to protect them. With a brush, paint a circle of oil around plants that have been attacked.

It is not too late to plant out perennials.

Don't forget to put twigs around young plants to protect them.

Hotbed:
1. *Sloping, detachable protective pane.*
2. *Top layer of compost, sieved on the surface.*
3. *Layer of fresh horse manure, well packed down and left to ferment.*

Plant out young plants grown indoors last year and plants received from friends. Give your deciduous plants a feed of special fertilizer.

Remember the lawn: This is the time to aerate the lawn and feed it a little lime. Cut it for the first time when the new shoots reach a height of 4 in (10cm).

Flowering plants: Sow annuals between April and May and

plant your dahlias, gladioli and begonias. Your of geraniums and greenhouse plants can go out after the last ground frosts.

Spring pruning: Pinch out your currant bushes, cut back vine shoots and prune new growth on pear and apple espaliers.

Summer.

The lawn: Feed the lawn with a natural fertilizer. It needs regular cutting and watering during dry spells. Water the compost heap from time to time.

Flowering plants: From time to time loosen the soil between the plants. Feed the weaker ones with plant fertilizer.

Water young plants and those you have planted out when they need it. Tie up any clumps of perennials which have begun to take over.

Take particular care of the plants on your terrace – plant out the flowers in pots, fertilize and water.

Fill your hanging baskets and window boxes – water daily and feed with a liquid fertilizer once a week.

Remove dead heads regularly from your annual plants and roses. This will encourage them to keep flowering right through the season.

Don't forget to make full use of all medicinal and edible plants. Use your herbs in the kitchen, make fruit squash, as well as jams and preserves for the freezer. Pick your apples and peaches before they become "woolly".

The hedge: Don't forget to prune the hedge in August.

IS IT NECESSARY TO USE PESTICIDES?

In days gone by, pesticides and herbicides didn't exist and our ancestors managed to protect their crops quite adequately from predators. Remember the scarecrow?

Since the last war, a wide range of pesticides has come onto the market and not a single species of insect has disappeared since they have been in use.

The harmful effects of these miracle products by far outweigh their short-term advantages. Birds and butterflies are being poisoned and are beginning to disappear.

People are now realizing that the natural balance is the best guarantee against all kinds of infestation. We can best maintain this balance by growing a wide variety of plants. However, there are still times when we feel the need to intervene to combat unexpected pests. We can do this quite adequately by using natural products without any need for pesticides.

Instead of using a complete or selective weedkiller on your gravel, use boiling water, a blow lamp or a hot air paint stripper.

Use the simple methods of dealing with slugs and snails – the dish of beer, egg shells, wood shavings or cinders. Blackbirds and thrushes will give you a helping hand with the snails. Slugs love marigolds! Dot them about your flower-beds to act as "decoys".

Get rid of aphids by spraying with soapy water with added nicotine. Or, plant elder and use the leaves to make a spray. Chop enough of the leaves to fill a pan and simmer in 40 fl.oz (1l) water for half an hour. Dilute with 80 fl.oz (2l) cold water and spray on to the aphids. You can use rhubarb leaves instead of elder leaves. Both mixtures are safe for bees and will break down quickly in the soil. Be sure to use the mixture within twenty-four hours.

Use sulphur to treat plants affected by fungal diseases, and spray with copper sulphate to combat mildew. You can also combat mildew by spraying with used dishwashing water.

Every winter spray your fruit trees with a tar wash solution.

Destroy some of the larvae with an innocuous oily solution. Or use a preventive liquid manure fertilizer made from nettles. For the recipe see "My Tips" at the end of the chapter.

The golden rule for the use of commercial products is always to buy only natural products, i.e. products which do not have a chemical base.

This rule is as valid for fertilizers as for products to protect your plants.

I save all my earthenware pots and all my wooden boxes. They can be used for transporting plants or for additions to the pond.

I find old pallets useful for doing odd jobs in the garden.

If I had a larger garden, I would grow a patch of "wonder" nettles. Butterflies lay their eggs on nettles – especially in a sunny position. For the moment I get my supply of nettles when I go walking in the country. Here is the recipe for liquid manure made from fermented nettles: Pick 2 lb (1 kg) of nettles, without roots, and place them in a weighted sack. Place the sack inside a container filled with 20 pints (10 l) of rainwater. Cover, leaving a gap to allow the air to circulate. After a week or two the liquid manure is ready. Use the liquid manure mixed with water in a ratio of 1 part manure to 20 parts water.

My tips.

I have put an electric pump on the rainwater tank. The garden hose is plugged into the circuit. I can water the garden as often as necessary at no extra cost.

I use secateurs on the end of a pole to finish pruning my old pear tree.

I keep a stock of strong, old polythene bags for bringing back compost and manure when I go into the country.

I always keep a seed tray, a bag, a collapsible spade, a pair of secateurs and a pocket knife in the boot of my car so that I don't miss any golden opportunities when I'm out in the country. But remember it is illegal to dig up any wild plants and even to pick the flowers of certain protected species.

USEFUL ADDRESSES.

Peter Beales Roses : London Road, Attleborough, Norfolk NR17 1AY. Tel: 0953 454707
Specialise in old-fashioned climbing and shrub roses.

John Chambers' Wild Flower Seeds : 15 Westleigh, Barton Seagrave, Kettering, Northamptonshire NN15 5AJ. Tel: 0933 681632

Cranborne Manor Garden Centre : Cranborne, Dorset BH21 5PP. Tel: 0725 4248
Specialise in old-fashioned climbing and shrub roses.

Chase Organics Ltd : Coombelands House, Coombelands Lane, Addlestone, Weybridge, Surrey KT15 1HY. Tel: 0932 858511
Suppliers of organic seeds and composts.

The Henry Doubleday Research Association : Ryton-on-Dunsmore, Coventry, West Midlands CV8 3LG. Tel: 0203 303517
A registered charity that carries out research into organic gardening and farming. Also offers an organic gardening advice service for members. Membership details available on request.

Eden Nurseries : Rectory Lane, Old Bolingbroke, Spilsby, Lincolnshire. Tel: 079 03 583
Specialise in old English varieties of apple trees.

The Soil Association : 86 Colston Street, Bristol, Avon BS1 5BB. Tel: 0272 290661

Stapeley Water Gardens Ltd : London Road, Stapeley, Nantwich, Cheshire CW5 7JL. Tel: 0270 623868
Specialise in native wetland and water plants.

Suffolk Herbs : Sawyers Farm, Little Cornard, Sudbury, Suffolk CO10 0NY. Tel: 0787 227247
Specialise in wild flower and herb seeds.

The Wild Flower Society : 69 Outwoods Road, Loughborough, Leicestershire.

FURTHER READING.

Chris Baines: *How to Make a Wildlife Garden,* Elm Tree Books, 1985

John Chambers: *Wild Flower Garden,* Elm Tree Books, 1987

Laurence D. Hills: *The Good Fruit Guide,* Henry Doubleday Research Association.

International Bee Research Association: *Garden Plants Valuable to Bees,* International Bee Research Association, 1981

John Killingbeck: *Creating and Maintaining a Garden to Attract Butterflies,* National Association for Environmental Education, 1985

Roy Lacey: *Organic Gardening,* David & Charles, 1988

Helen McEwan: *Seed Growers' Guide to Herbs and Wild Flowers,* Suffolk Herbs, 1982

John Stevens: *The National Trust Book of Wildflower Gardening,* Dorling Kindersley, 1987

Sue Stickland: *The Organic Garden,* Hamlyn, 1987

Urban Wildlife Group: *Gardening for Wildlife,* Urban Wildlife Group, 1986

In addition, *Organic Gardening,* a monthly magazine, is available from newsagents or by subscription from: Organic Gardening Editorial & Subscription Office, P.O. Box 4, Wivelscombe, Taunton, Somerset TA4 2QY. Tel: 0984 23998.

GARDEN LAYOUT FOR THE ENTHUSIAST.

This is a tiny town garden which faces south-east. It is only about 18 ft (5.5m) wide by 50 ft (15m) long and is surrounded by high walls. At the bottom there is a tool shed and a hundred-year-old cherry tree (A).

In the right hand corner there is a clump of lilac (B).

In front of the house is a terrace 8 ft (2.5m) wide.

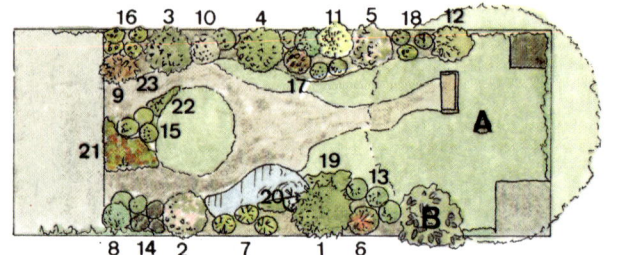

You have lots of ideas and love planting things. So what can you do?

Benoit Choteau suggests you look in your plant catalogues:

1. A dwarf tree, or a dwarf bush conifer, for example: Pinus mugo "Gnom".

2. A spring-flowering shrub with a pyramid-shaped habit, for example: Prunus "Kanzan".

3. An evergreen shrub with an erect habit, 5 ft (1.5m) after ten years, with greenish-blue foliage, for example: Juniperus chinensis "Pyramidalis".

4. Tree with decorative foliage, with a pyramid-shaped habit, for example: Carpinus betulus "Fastigiata".

5. A spring-flowering shrub 10-15 ft (3-4m), with a narrow habit, for example: Prunus Amanogawa".

6. Shrub, 8 ft (2.5m), with tufted branches, with decorative bark in winter, for example: Cornus alba "Sibirica".

7. Three clumps of grasses or bamboo, 8 ft (2.5m) high, for example: Miscanthus sinensis "Silver Feather".

8. Small evergreen shrub with white flowers, for example: Osmarea burkwoodii.

9. Shrub, 3 ft (1m), with decorative serrated foliage, for example: Acer palmatum "Dissectum Atropurpureum".

10. Spring-flowering decorative shrub, 4 ft (1.2m), pale yellow foliage, for example: Weigela florida "Variegata".

11. Spring-flowering shrub, bushy habit and slender branches, for example: Cytisus praecox.

12. Evergreen shrub with shiny green foliage, for example: Aucuba japonica.

13. Small evergreen shrub with delicate flowers, for example: Viburnum davidii.

14. A small evergreen shrub with decorative fruits in winter, for example: Pernettya mucronata.

15. Small evergreen shrub, 1½ ft (50cm), for example: Berberis thumbergii "Nana".

16. Small shrub, 1½ ft (50cm), with an abundance of yellow flowers from May to August, for example: Potentilla fruticosa "Yellow Queen".

17. Summer-flowering shrub with rounded habit, crimson flowers, for example: Spiraea bumalda "Goldflame".

18. Spring-flowering, evergreen shrub, with blue-black berries later in the season, 4 ft (1.2m), for example: Mahonia aquifolium.

19. Heather, for example: Erica tetralix.

20. Decorative herbs, under 1 ft (30cm), for example: Convallaria majalis (Lily-of-the-valley).

21. A variety of perennials that like sun and some shade.

22. A variety of heathers.

23. A few low-growing perennials.

GARDEN LAYOUT FOR THE IDLE GARDENER.

The garden of this modern house faces south-east. It is 26 ft (8m) wide by 40 ft (12m) long and is enclosed by wire fencing. A coniferous hedge of thujas has recently been planted 2½ ft (75cm) in front of this. There is a sparse lawn in the central area of the garden, the walls of the house overlooking the garden are bare and there is a terrace between the house and the garden.

I asked Mrs van Horenbeeck, a landscape gardener, to plan the layout of an imaginative garden that must be extremely pleasant to be in and yet easy to maintain.

This is what she suggested:

1. The existing thujas have been cut to make a low hedge.

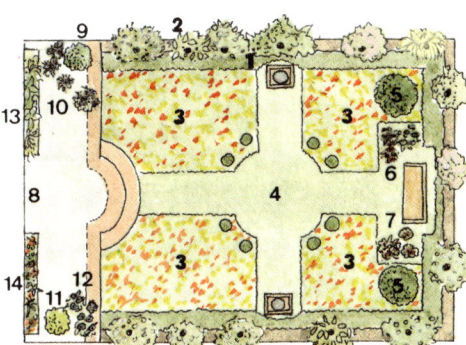

2. Behind them different sorts of shrubs, suitable for quickset hedges, have been planted separately and form a flowering hedge, for example: Viburnum, hawthorn, blackthorn, laburnum.

3. The lawn has become wild grass full of all sorts of flowers through which pathways have been cut the width of a motor mower.

4. Two small conifers or evergreen shrubs are trimmed to a rounded shape.

5. Here, plant a few attractive, summer-flowering deciduous shrubs, between 1½-3 ft (50cm-1m) high, for example: Hydrangea.

6. Here, arrange pots containing a variety of bright scented annuals, for example: Nicotiana.

7. Train fast-growing varieties of climber against the side of the house, for example: Hydrangea petiolaris, Virginia creeper.

8. Here you could stand an attractive earthenware pot containing a greenhouse plant, which you bring in during winter, for example: Laurel.

9. Here, arrange a selection of azaleas and dwarf rhododendrons.

10. Plant a graceful, spring-flowering shrub, for example: Ligustrum (privet) or symphoricarpos.

11. For this spot choose a small, summer-flowering, shrub, for example: Weigela, hypericum, euonymus.

12. In this container, plant a selection of ferns and bulbs, for example: Hostas, agapanthus.

13. Plant a few sun-loving hardy perennials, for example: Asters, antirrhinums and a few rock plants.

GARDEN LAYOUT FOR THE OCCASIONAL GARDENER.

This town garden is extremely long, 82 ft (25m), and only 20 ft (6m) wide. It faces north-west and is surrounded by walls 8 ft (2.5m) high. It has been neglected but a few trees have survived:

A. At the bottom, a fifty-year-old field maple.
B. On the left, about half-way down, a group of apricot trees.
C. Among them, a neglected espalier pear tree.
D. On the right, currant bushes.

There is a wide terrace between the house and the garden.

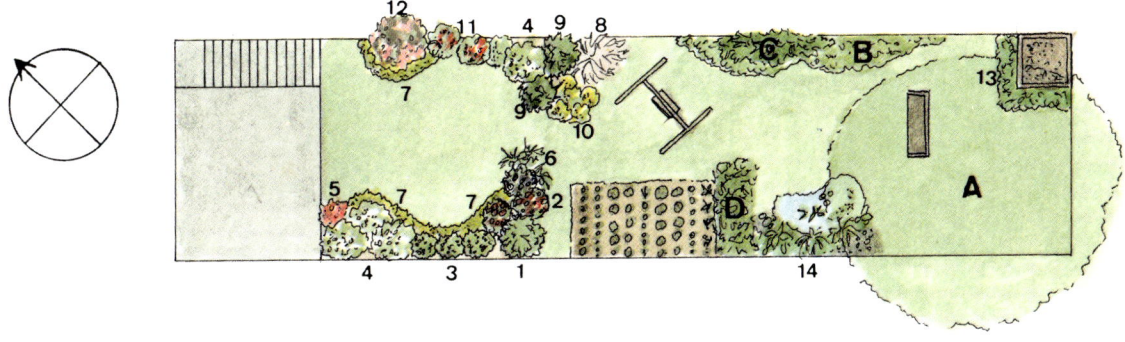

I asked Benoit Choteau, botanist and landscape gardener, to design a layout. Here are his suggestions:

1. Here, plant a conifer with a narrow habit and greenish-blue foliage, for example: Picea omorika.

2. Plant summer-flowering shrubs, 6 ft (2m) high, for example: Hibiscus syriacus.

3. Here, side by side, two small shrubs with pink blossom in spring, for example: Chaenomeles speciosa.

4. In this corner, three shrubs with white, scented blossom in spring, for example: Philadelphus coronarius.

5. In front of these, a bush with greenish-brown or reddish foliage, for example: Weigela florida variegata.

6. A small, evergreen shrub, for example: Juniperus sabina tamariscifolia.

7. In front of all these shrubs, a small, narrow border with a variety of shade-loving perennials, for example: Geranium pratense "Johnson's Blue", chamomile, campanula, mallow.

8. On this side, plant a spring-flowering shrub, 10-12 ft (3-4m), with light foliage, for example: Tamarix tetrandra.

9. Next to this, two evergreen shrubs with scented flowers, for example: Osmanthus delavayi.

10. In front of these, a few, small evergreen bush shrubs, for example: Hypericum x inodorum "Elstead".

11. Here, a shrub, 3-6 ft (1-2m), with berries between September and December, for example: Callicarpa bodinieri giraldii.

12. Next to this, a spring-flowering shrub with a column-like habit, for example: Malus "Van Eseltine".

13. A shrub with light foliage to conceal the compost container, for example: Ligustrum.

14. Near the pond, plant shade-loving marsh plants and grasses, for example: Astilbe, Osmunda regalis, Carex elata "Aurea".

Other interesting books from Exley Publications:

The Illustrated Gardener's Notebook. £7.99 (including VAT, hardback). These 94-page notebooks are illustrated with the most beautiful full-colour paintings throughout on the theme of plants and gardening. They provide ample space for the owner to plan ahead, make notes of successful experiments in the garden, record useful information, or for any other use. Each spread has a short quotation relating to the theme from such well-known writers as Oscar Wilde, H.E. Bates and Walt Whitman. A superb and unique gift for any gardener.

In the same series, **The Illustrated Cook's Notebook** shows the beauty of food from tarts and pasta to herbs and the main tools used in kitchens. Any cook will be delighted with this gift.

The Illustrated Gardening Address Book and **The Illustrated Flower-Arranging Address Book.** £5.99 (including VAT, hardback). New from Exley Publications, these two titles form part of this superb series of full-colour address books, elegantly bound with picture covers, with generous address spaces. Artists featured in the series include Van Gogh, Manet, Breughel, Stubbs, F. Gordon Crosbie and "Spy". Other titles include: Golf, Horses, Motoring, Sailing, Tea and Wine.

Also available are **The Illustrated Flower-Arranging Day Book** and **The Illustrated Gardening Day Book.** These dateless diaries have 52 full colour pictures (one for each full week of the year). £8.99 (including VAT, hardback).

The Crazy World of Gardening. £3.99 (hardback). Ninety pages of riotous fun on the subject of gardening and gardeners. This is a perfect gift for anyone who has ever wrestled with a lawn-mower that refused to start, over-watered a neighbour's pot plant or been assaulted by a rose-bush.

Listening to Nature. £6.99 (paperback). This major new work by the famous American naturalist Joseph Cornell is designed to help you deepen your awareness of nature. Cornell says that even amidst the most stunning scenery and marvellous plants and animals many people cannot relax because they are too attuned to the bustle of the cities. Based on thoughts, poems and quotations of the great naturalists of the past, Cornell provides a series of exercises in a day-by-day format over a month to allow you to slow down and merge into the peace of nature so encouraging the birds and animals to lose their fear and the wonders of the wild to appear. Stunningly illustrated in colour throughout with photographs by the brilliant nature photographer John Hendrickson, this is a superb gift for anyone who loves the natural world.

Sharing Nature with Children. £5.99 (paperback). A collection of over forty games which children can play in the country, in city parks and in their own gardens. Compiled by a well-known naturalist, Joseph Cornell, these games are great fun. But they also bring a real understanding of such phenomena as camouflage and radar and will widen the children's awareness of the natural world around them.

Cry for our Beautiful World. £7.99 (hardback). This book was compiled from the writings and paintings of children from over 70 countries. Gathered from around the world, this is a passionate cry that we should see what is happening to the natural world before it is too late. Everywhere around them, these children see the creeping spread of humanity's destructive activities; they do not want to be the generation that wipes out the blue whale or see the last gorilla in the wild. They *love* nature – they treasure it. And they want people to change their ways before it is too late for the animal world.

Discovering Nature. £9.99 (hardback). A polar bear in the Arctic is nature. So is a rare orchid in the tropical rainforest or a zebra on the African plains. But nature is also a dandelion, an egg from a supermarket or a rotting apple. The great feature of the second list is that you can find them all at home! This book is about discovering nature's surprises – without travel, without expensive apparatus and without complicated scientific words. And it's great fun with some of the experiments seeming like magic tricks, with results that can be guaranteed. We suspect that some of the experiments may tempt older readers to try them as well! This is the first children's nature book of its kind – nothing quite like it has ever appeared before. You'll learn a lot while having fun – so let nature surprise you.

The Precious Present by Dr. Spencer Johnson. £6.99 (hardback). This intriguing little book is a simple story about the secret of happiness – as told by an old man to a young boy. Beautifully scripted in calligraphy on parchment paper, this is a gift to treasure (and ponder) for a lifetime.

A Gift of Flowers by Frances Berrill & Helen Exley. £1.99 (hardback). An unusual gift book which features "photograms" of rare leaves, grasses and plants coupled with poems and quotations celebrating the beauty of flowers and of the English countryside. Because no negatives are used in the process, each picture is unique and can never be re-created. "A delight to the eye ... a treasure trove." *The Flower Arranger.*

Give Happiness a Chance by Phil Bosmans. £5.99 (paperback). This quiet reflective book has sold more than 2,000,000 copies. The author is a Belgian who works with deprived groups and, a few years ago, started a phone-in service for the lonely. His messages were picked up by a local publisher and became a smash hit. Bosmans talks about the value of simple things, about human relationships, about the people who don't give, don't care. He talks about possessions – and the poverty outside the First World. A deeply religious person, Bosmans' language is direct and blunt, but the book speaks to everybody, religious or agnostic. Time and again, people tell us what a wonderful book this is, and recommend it to their friends.

These books make super presents. Order them from your local bookseller or from Exley Publications Ltd, Dept BP, 16 Chalk Hill, Watford, Herts WD1 4BN. (Please send £1.00 to cover post and packing.) Exley Publications reserves the right to show new retail prices on books which may vary from those previously advertised.